Your Retirement Made Simple

Publisher's Disclaimer

While the publisher and coauthors have used their best efforts in preparing this book, they make no representations or warranties with respect to the accuracy or completeness of the contents of this book. Nothing in this book should be construed as offering legal, tax, or financial advice. No warranty may be created or extended by sales representatives or written sales materials. The advice and strategies contained herein may not be suitable for your situation. You should consult with a professional where appropriate. Neither the publisher nor the authors shall be liable for any loss of profit or any other commercial damages, including but not limited to special, incidental, consequential or other damages.

Created and produced in Atlanta, Georgia, USA

First Edition, Volume 1

Table of Contents

Introduction V

Chapter 1 1
Your Retirement Made Simple - in a Nutshell
Timothy J. Turner, JD

Chapter 2 27
Tips on How to "Make YOUR Retirement Simple"
Timothy J. Turner, JD

Chapter 3 63
Life is More Than a Paycheck
Chuck Price, CRFA, CSA

Chapter 4 97
The Exponential Power of Two
Daryl Shankland & Buddy Nidey

Chapter 5 159
Increase Your Retirement Fund at No Cost
Joe Pereira

iv

Introduction

"Everything should be made as 'simple' as possible, but not simpler."

- Albert Einstein

This book is called **"Your Retirement Made Simple"** because I have seen too many people make retirement planning out to be "too complicated". It's always easy to use "technobabble" and "jargon" to make things hard to understand. But it's actually difficult to avoid using technical terms to convey information in simple terms that people understand. It takes special skill to make something understandable without dumbing it down so much that too much information is lost. And I think that is the gist of what Albert Einstein was talking about.

Let me be clear that I am not a financial planner or a financial advisor. I have never sold any financial products or services. My experience has been in developing software for the financial industry – financial advisors, planners, and financial companies. So I have been able to be an "outsider looking in" at what goes on in the financial industry. This has given me insight into what is "complicated" and what could be made "simpler".

Have you read a financial or retirement book and never finished it? Was it because it was too complicated to understand and left you with a headache? Or was it because it was just plain boring and too long?

Regardless, with this book we have tried to collate some valuable expertise while "keeping it simple" and understandable. In fact, the book is based on a short interview format rather than as a long boring educational read. We are hoping that this format is more digestible, easier-to-understand, and "simpler" to read.

In fact, the content in this book came from interviews that I did with each author. In keeping with the book theme, it is the "simplest" way to draw good content from busy experts quickly.

This book is also fairly short. I believe many books are too long and that it turns off the reader. We wanted this book to be something you can read quickly without you getting bored and putting it down to never finish.

I've also elicited the help from four financial advisors that are actual practitioners of varying types. In this way you get a more well-rounded view of how you can improve your retirement finances. All four of the other authors have used our RetirementView software with their clients, and that's how I know them… through their relationship with Torrid Technologies.

To introduce you to the other authors of this book….

Chuck Price, CRFA, CSA is President & Wealth Manager of Price Financial Group Wealth Management, Inc. a Registered Investment Advisory Firm (RIA) who for over 40 years has worked with hundreds of clients from coast to coast, employing comprehensive planning services and has developed strategies with the goals of helping clients increase income, reduce taxation, and never run out of money in retirement. He is the Author of the book "Investing Simplified" and is co-host on the longest running Live Financial Talk Show in America with a Financial Advisor, Estate Planning Attorney and a CPA, broadcasted out of Portland, Oregon every Saturday 8am PST and on the web: www.InvestingSimplifiedRadio.com and his motto, "What You Don't Know Can Hurt You"

Daryl Shankland has been guiding clients in their investment decisions since 1980, encompassing both good times and bad. Her broadcasting background has helped her communicate complex, quickly changing information to clients in a manner that they can understand. Daryl has been a frequent commentator on financial matters on both television and radio. She served as branch manager of the Quincy, Illinois Smith Barney branch for many years before leaving to start her own firm. With her deep experience in management and client portfolio structuring, she understands how emotions can take their toll and how critical it is to trust your financial advisor.

As an Accountant and a graduate of the College of Financial Planning in Denver, Colorado, **Buddy Nidey** applies his strong analytical to his work as an investment advisor representative. He enjoys coordinating clients' investment portfolios with solid financial planning that takes income taxes, diversification and safety into consideration. Bud also assists clients with income tax preparation, health, life and long term care insurance as part of his financial consulting services.

Together, **Daryl** and **Buddy** work to educate their nearby communities with outreach on various topics of financial literacy. They conduct frequent workshops on Social Security Maximization, Taxes in Retirement, and Retirement Income Planning in public venues and for area businesses. They are both members of the Society for Financial Awareness, a not for profit organization dedicated to financial education.

Joe Pereira supports the retirement lifestyle plans of pre-retirees and retirees with financial planning strategies that focus on growth with preservation of capital. As President of Legacy Planning, Inc. he has personally assisted hundreds of families to wisely protect their assets and pay less income tax along the way. Joe has over 30 years of accounting and planning experience. His firm is based out of Miami, Florida.

Each one of us has some valuable insights to share with you in your journey to reach "YOUR Retirement Made Simple". We hope you enjoy this book. Please visit our website at www.YourRetirementMadeSimple.com to give us your feedback and also to download some free resources related to the book.

Thanks and Happy Planning!

Timothy J. Turner, JD
Founder of Torrid Technologies

x

Chapter 1

Your Retirement Made Simple - in a Nutshell

Timothy J. Turner, JD

First I'd like to introduce myself. My name is Tim Turner and I'm the founder of Torrid Technologies. I'm kind of a software nerd and a programmer, but I'm also an expert in financial and retirement planning. I've developed a program called RetirementView that helps baby boomers, business owners, and seniors to quickly and easily build their own retirement picture so that they can have peace of mind about their retirement finances and avoid running out of money during retirement. I've also helped design financial planning systems for fortune 500 companies like Pacific Life, MassMutual, AXA, TIAA-CREF, and JANUS Mutual Funds

Who should read this book, who is it for, and how will it help you?

Tim Turner: I wanted to start off by mentioning a survey by Transamerica Center for Retirement Studies. In the survey, they surveyed seniors about their fears. And their number one fear was running out of money in retirement. Now this is surprising because this was rated number one even over dying! So more people are afraid of running out of money than they are of dying. So this sets the context for our book and why we are writing it.

This book is really for anyone that is starting to think about their retirement in terms of finances and saving for retirement, or that is already retired and needs to manage it. If you're a baby boomer or a senior frankly anyone that is planning to retire and wants to make sure that they are financially secure, then this book is for you.

If you're like me at all, no one ever talked to me about retirement or even about saving money. It's not something that comes naturally to people without learning more about it, and so I wanted to share what I know with you so that I can help you in your journey to have a decent retirement.

If you are a millennial or just early in your career, the longer you wait to save for retirement the harder it's going to be, so I encourage you to start early and just put a percentage of your pay away. Start with five or 10%, whatever you think you can do, but if you do that starting early, then you'll be surprised how much money you can accumulate for retirement and just 10 or 20 years.

If you were a Gen X or a GEN Y generation, then you're kind of in the middle of your career. You should already be saving for retirement. If you're not, you need to get started as soon as possible. If you are already saving, then you need to start running some calculations that show you whether you're on track and whether you should be saving more. Running some numbers can help you to direct what you're doing so that you can get on a path toward success. I'm going to share with you some tips on how you can do that.

If you are a baby boomer and you have not yet retired, then you are right there in those last few years that are so key towards planning your retirement finances. With respect to retirement you need to figure out what you're going to get from Social Security. You need to be saving and you need to be planning. You need to be working on when you think you can retire and start planning around that.

And these are not easy things to figure out. Hopefully through this book you'll learn some ways that will improve what you're going to be doing, as well as some strategies that will help keep you from running out of money in retirement.

If you are already retired, then it's important for you to track your expenses, your income streams, and your investments, so that you make sure you don't run out of money when you're retired. It's a balancing act between spending your money and growing your money, and it's often not easy to do. But hopefully we will give you some strategies that will help you maneuver through the minefield of retirement.

The last group that we help are financial advisors and insurance agents who work with their clients on their retirement. They use our software to help create retirement pictures for their clients that are easy to understand and that help them have strong conversations about what planning needs to be done to secure their client's retirement future.

What is your background and how did you get involved with retirement planning?

Tim Turner: When I was with a student at Boston University studying electrical engineering, we took a course on the time value of money called engineering economy. In this course we had a professor who talked

4

about saving in a 401(k) plan. As students we didn't know what a 401(k) plan was. We had no clue.

But our professor wanted to show us a real world example that would let us use the calculations that we learned as well as to see the benefit of saving for retirement in our jobs. So he tried to run a hypothetical by saying that all of you will get a job and let's say you make $40,000 a year (note: this was back in 1989). And let's suppose you save 6% of your pay and your company matches 3% of your pay. That means your employer will give you some free money if you in turn save for your own retirement. So it was like an incentive to save for retirement. And what if you're in this job for 30 or 40 years and let's say you get a raise of 3% every year, so that your contributions go up every year. And let's say that you get an investment return of a certain amount save 5%. How much will you be able to save for retirement by the time you're 65?

He taught us the calculations involved in this example and how to make them. And we used that to run some numbers with respect to saving in the 401(k) plan. After running these calculations, he proved to us that under certain circumstances and average investment returns, we could actually save over $1 million by the time that we retired.

Everyone in the class got really excited because we never knew anything about a 401(k) plan, and we didn't know anything about investing either. So the idea that we could just work a regular engineering job and accumulate so much investment money for retirement was an incredible eye-opening experience.

When I graduated and started working my first engineering job at a big firm, I signed up for the 401(k) plan right off the bat as soon as they would let me do it. And I merely saved for my retirement as soon as I got out of college. Now at some point I switched to a different job at another company, and I had to wait a few months to join the 401(k) plan. We had an enrollment meeting where you go to sign up for the 401(k) plan.

At that meeting, no one could tell me how much I should save for retirement. I asked the human resources person all kinds of questions like how much should I be saving. Do you know how long our money will last in retirement? And what kind of investment return should we expect? And all they could say is "Sorry we can't help you". So I worked on a Microsoft Excel spreadsheet to try to run some numbers and I shared that with my co-workers who thought it was just OK. I then decided I was going to program something at home that could do more detailed calculations and that was when Torrid Technologies was born.

I bought a Mac LC II computer, a printer, and a software development system called Prograph which has now long been discontinued back in the late 1990s. I also started using America Online and CompuServe because the Internet hadn't taken off yet. So I worked full-time all day and then in the evenings I would program on the Mac and work on the first version of our software, which we called $401k Planner. I sold it on America Online and

CompuServe as shareware asking people to send in $10 if they liked the program. I didn't know anything about running a business. This was way back in 1993. That first year I had only seven people send me a check for a grand total of $70 in revenue. Quite humble beginnings for a company.

What's the number one thing you would advise people when talking about planning for retirement?

Tim Turner: Well, the number one thing I would tell people that are not yet retired is that you need to start saving for retirement as soon as possible. If you start when you get out of college in your first job, assuming that you have a retirement plan there, then you'll never miss the percentage of money that you put away for retirement. But if you wait five or 10 years and then sign up for retirement deductions, you will essentially feel like you're having a pay cut to start saving for retirement and that will be a lot more difficult. In other words, if you wait you will feel the reduction in your paycheck, versus doing it when you first start working.

So wherever you are, whether you're at the beginning of your career or middle of your career or end of your career, you need to be saving for retirement. You need to put a percentage of your income away for your retirement savings, and you need to do it every week and every month that you get a paycheck. If you don't do this, then there's no way you're going to wait till you're 60 retiring at 65 and be able to save enough money to pay for all the needs you are going to have during your retirement years.

The second most important thing that you need to be doing besides putting away money for retirement is to do some calculations to determine how much you'll be able to save. You also need to figure out what your expenses will be in retirement and what other income streams that you have so that you can reconcile all of these things in one picture. In doing that exercise you'll be able to see any issues before they crop up. For example, you can look out and see if you're going to run out of money and then make adjustments to correct that course and improve your retirement.

In this book we're going to share some strategies on how you can do this more efficiently and effectively. Of course anyone trying out our RetirementView software from Torrid Technologies can easily put all their information into one picture and see whether they're going to run out of money, as well as how much they're going to accumulate for retirement.

Once someone has already begun saving for retirement, how do you actually help them at that point?

Tim Turner: We can help them with several issues that they may have. One that we've already mentioned is, will you have enough money to retire? You may still be working and you're trying to figure out when you can retire. Can I retire at 62 or 65 or 68? Will I have enough money at that point to retire? And you need to run some calculations to figure all that out!

The main issue with this is the problem of putting all of the variables involved in these calculations into one understandable picture. So that includes, for example, if you're married you need to include your spouse. If you're married and they work and they have a retirement plan at work, then you need to include all of those financial aspects into the calculations which adds a second dimension to what you have to figure out.

So if someone is already saving in their retirement plan at work or on their own or even both, we help them by getting all of their financial variables into one picture in one place that they can see visually and know how all of the pieces and parts are going to play out on the chessboard. This is something that's not easy to do without using a good software program.

Even if you're amazing with Microsoft Excel, it's nearly impossible to do what we've done in a mere spreadsheet. It requires real software programming to include all of the variables. It requires algorithms to do certain calculations. So it's essential that you do some basic planning.

What is the most important thing about helping people develop their retirement plans?

Tim Turner: In my mind, the most important thing is to help people quickly and easily generate their own retirement picture – basically their own retirement calculations. Their own retirement snapshot. It's a peek into their retirement future and whether they're going to run out of money. But if the exercise is too time-consuming and too complicated, then most people won't get through it and get any value out of it, so it's got to be pretty simple to do.

And that's what our software does... it makes it very simple for anyone to build their own retirement picture. We've got 80 and 90-year-old people that didn't grow up using a computer that have gotten our software and been able to enter their information and track their retirement finances. This is something anyone can do regardless of how good you are with the computer. If you can fill in the blanks on a form, then you can build your own retirement picture using our RetirementView software. The software itself is doing all of the complicated calculations in the background.

You just brought up 80 and 90-year-old people... Isn't that a little too old to be planning for retirement?

No because even at that age you still have to plan out your expenses and investments, as well as how you're going to manage your income streams. I agree that this book isn't perfectly geared towards older seniors, but I brought it up just as an example to let everyone know how easy it is to use the RetirementView software. And even if someone is 80 years old, they can use the software to enter their information and to track their investments and expenses to make sure that they don't run out of money.

So the RetirementView system will be useful to people of any age. But the sweet spot I agree is definitely the baby boomers and people recently retired that want to make sure that they're on track in that critical period right before retirement as well as right after they've started retirement.

What is the big overall benefit to building your own retirement picture in doing some retirement calculations?

In my own life my father's mother, whose name was Eula, had Alzheimer's and ended up in a nursing home for over 10 years. My grandfather had already passed away and my aunt basically visited her in the nursing home almost every day. But it took a lot of planning in order to provide for her care for all of those years. So it's a very personal thing when you have grandparents or parents go through health issues in retirement. And even if they don't go through health issues, you may see them in retirement struggling to make ends meet and it's kind of heartbreaking. They are "living on a fixed income" as we have heard many times.

On the other side of my family, my wife's grandmother at the time I'm writing this is 101 years old and living in a nursing home in Alabama. And again, without a lot of advanced planning, she probably wouldn't be able to afford where she is now. They really take decent care of her, and she's joyful there. And she just is not able to live alone anymore.

So it's not just the living expenses in retirement, traveling around, maintaining a home, those sorts of thoughts that people have about retirement, but it's also the health issues that crop up, as well as care in the home and care out of the home if you have to go to a facility. These are all very important issues that you need to take into consideration when planning your finances in retirement.

Now let's assume that someone is saving for retirement and they're taking the matter seriously, if they decide they want to work with someone like an advisor, what are the biggest issues that they have to deal with?

Tim Turner: Well one of the biggest issues is finding someone that you can trust. Trust seems to be hard to come by in this day and age. And a big part of that is due to Bernie Madoff. As we all know Bernie Madoff propagated one of the largest Ponzi schemes ever in the United States and probably the world.

He faked investment statements and fraudulently showed people that they were getting incredible returns, when in fact he wasn't investing the money at all, but was spending it on his own lavish lifestyle. And he didn't just defraud a few hundred people… it was thousands of people.   And these were smart and successful people, not just average Joes. There were even foundations that he claimed to invest their endowments.

I call this the "Bernie Madoff Effect", and it permeates a lot of people's thinking when they even consider working with a financial advisor. The first thing in their mind is "how do I know this guy isn't just going to steal all my money?" And that's a legitimate concern given all of the Ponzi schemes that keep cropping up in the news lately.

One of the things that you can do if you're concerned about this is to understand how you should work with the financial advisor. If you're going to have a financial advisor handle your investments and decide where you're going to be invested, I would suggest that you have your financial advisor manage your money and your accounts at what's called a "custodian". So for example you could have an account at E*TRADE or TD Ameritrade, or Charles Schwab. And if they have the money there, you sign an agreement that says the advisor can only take out their fees. They're not able to withdraw your funds in whole. So they can't just start writing themselves checks out of your accounts. They can only withdraw their investment management fees which are typically around 1% or so depending on who is managing your account.

If you start to work with a financial advisor and they ask you to roll your money over or write a check out to their own firm name, that's when you should at least be really suspicious. Because if you do that they're just putting it into one of their firm's accounts and they may have a lot more ability to remove funds than you really want to give them.

So trust is a really big issue these days. And even if you do have a financial advisor, it's important that you run your own numbers at home. You may not want to just blindly trust your advisor. My advice is to trust, but verify. Keep an idea of what your finances are on your own. Run your own retirement calculations and build your own retirement picture. This will help you not only to be more intelligent about your situation, but that in turn will help you be able to make better decisions.

Of course, if you have a financial advisor, including one of my co-authors, you can certainly have them build your retirement picture for you and discuss it with you. They all use our RetirementView software in their practices.

The financial industry marketplace is constantly changing both in terms of companies, mutual funds, as well as laws and taxation, how is an individual supposed to keep up with all of it and manage their own retirement?

This is a common question that I get. But let me give this caveat first... that we don't give any actual financial advice or legal advice. Even though I'm an attorney, we just offer our software for people to use in figuring out their retirement picture. We will help you use the program and enter all of your information. But neither Torrid Technologies nor myself can give real "financial advice" to you. To get that you must go to a financial professional.

Since the financial Industry is constantly in flux, it is important for you to look at your picture on a regular basis. When you get your investment statements, you need to revisit your retirement picture and look at your expenses as well, and make sure that you're still on track for retirement. You need to make sure that the projections show that you're not going to run out of money. And if for some reason it does show a problem, then you need to be able to make subtle changes that should help you avoid those problems. The only way to do that is to test different what if scenarios in order to determine what changes you should be making.

Maybe you are not retired yet and you need to consider saving more money. Or maybe you need to change your investment mix that you're getting returns without getting big losses as well. Perhaps you're not sure what age you can retire. And you need to figure out when you can retire or whether you need to work a couple more years. These are the types of questions that our software helps people answer.

So for the do-it-yourselfer, they get our software and often can at least figure out a roadmap that'll take them where they want to go in retirement. Now it doesn't tell you where to put your money. It doesn't tell you what investments to buy or what to invest in. You either have to figure that out on your own or hire a financial advisor to do it for you. That's one of the reasons I brought on several co-authors that may be able to help in this area.

Having worked with thousands of financial advisors over the years that use our software, I do highly recommend that you seek the advice of a professional. A true financial advisor can help you maneuver through the land mines of the stock market. That's something that I don't do. And that's something that our company is not involved with at this time. So if you would like someone to help you invest your money, manage your money, and help you with your investment accounts then I highly recommend a financial advisor.

I have seen a number of ads online and radio programs that talk about annuities. What is an annuity and why should I consider getting one?

That's a great question. An annuity is a product from an insurance company. The insurance company collects from you an initial premium and then promises you a return on your premium and possibly other promises as well including income for life. One benefit of that has been particularly popular is this income for life concept. The insurance term for it is typically "a lifetime income benefit rider".

If you get an annuity with a lifetime income rider, then it essentially is going to pay you for the rest of your life similar to a pension. This is why some people refer to a lifetime income benefit rider on an annuity as a "private pension". Unlike the stock market, most of the annuities promise that you cannot lose money. And that is an attractive feature to a person retired that doesn't want to be worried about the stock market tanking every week of their life.

There are number of ads online as well as radio shows that really put annuities into a negative light. They try to portray annuities as something terrible that only an idiot would do. And this is really not the case. The reason that most of these people are criticizing annuities is that they only do investments and want to sit on your nest egg and collect fees. So they don't sell annuities and thus they want to knock them as something that you shouldn't be doing. If you believe this, then in turn you're going to be attracted to that investment firm or person and consider them as a valuable source of information as well as investment advice. Or at least that's what I think their marketing theory is.

I would say just be careful with whomever you deal with and consider whether a source is biased or not. Annuity income definitely has a place in a person's retirement income picture. You can help avoid losses from the stock market that can devastate your retirement accounts. Too many people have retired thinking they are ready to go, but then the stock market tanks right after they retire and they realize that they have to go back to work. Annuities can help avoid this problem.

Again I want to emphasize that I am not a financial advisor and that you should seek the advice of a financial professional. This is why the other authors of this book have been invited to be a part of this project because they have insights to share with you that I cannot.

Can you tell us a little bit about the different retirement accounts that are available in the United States and some of the advantages and disadvantages of those accounts?

Yes of course I can. One of the issues with the retirement accounts, is that the names are a little technical. For example, one of the main plans is called a 401(k) plan. Most people would have a 401(k) plan through their work if they work for a private employer. This plan allows you to save in it on a before tax basis for the long-haul. In many cases an employer will offer matching funds. This is basically free money that they're giving you in return for saving into your 401(k) plan.

So for example, let's say you save 6% of your pay and you make $100,000 a year, you would be contributing $6,000 a year to your account. If your employer matches you 50% on the dollar, then they would be giving you an additional 3% of your pay, which would be another $3,000 to put into your account. Even if the investment selections in your 401(k) plan don't give you great investment returns you're essentially getting a 50% return on your investment just for saving in the plan when your employer offers these matching funds.

There are also solo 401(k) plans that are geared towards very small businesses. There is also a Roth 401(k) plan, which allows you to save after taxes into the plan, typically through an employer for those that offer this type of plan. This type of plan is relatively new and a lot of employers are not yet offering it. The nice thing about a Roth 401(k) is that when you get to retirement and withdraw the money there will be no taxes due. For a regular 401(k) plan, when you get to retirement you will owe ordinary income taxes on every withdrawal just as if it were given to you in a paycheck.

Many state and county governments offer what is called a 403(b) plan. It's very similar to the 401(k) plan but just typically offered by governments. For example, most teachers at public schools have access to a 403(b) plan through their school. Many times the choice of investments in these plans are not that great. If you have one of these plans, you may want to consult a financial advisor about other alternatives.

The other way to save for retirement is to use an IRA. One type of IRA is called the "Traditional IRA". The Traditional IRA lets you save for retirement before taxes. That means when you withdraw the money you will have to pay ordinary income taxes on it. It's important to know this because taxes may be going up in the future because of all the debts that our government has run up.

The other type of IRA account is called the "Roth IRA". You save into the Roth IRA using after tax funds. Thus, it does not reduce the taxes you owe in your current tax year (i.e. no deduction), but any money that you put into the Roth IRA account can be invested and grow tax-free until you need to withdraw it. When you finally do take the withdrawals in retirement, they are also tax free!

This is one of the reasons so many people like the Roth IRA. Being able to use the account for retirement without having to pay any taxes on it whatsoever is almost a deal that seems too good to be true! There are a number of advanced retirement planning techniques that take advantage of the Roth IRA. I'm not going to go into these here, but I would highly suggest you talk to a financial professional about how those might work for you.

Keep in mind that many times "politicians" in Washington D.C. have talked about taxing the Roth IRA and perhaps even the 401(k) plans as a way to reduce deficits.

This "changing of the rules" is not something most people want of course.

You might be wondering why everyone doesn't just use the Roth IRA for all of their retirement savings. First of all, you don't get any current tax deduction for saving into the Roth IRA. In addition there are income limits on the Roth IRA, which means that if you make over a certain amount of income then your contribution is limited or even not allowed.

For 2017, if you are under 50 the most you can save in a Roth IRA is $5,500. If you are 50 or over, you can save up to $6,500. In addition to those limits, if you are married filing jointly, you cannot contribute at all if your income is $196,000 or higher. (See appendix for additional information).

What are some of the big misconceptions when it comes to retirement planning?

I think one of the biggest misconceptions is that your investment return is the most important factor in accumulating money for retirement. After studying many retirement plans, I personally think the biggest factors include when you start saving, how much you save, and the effects of inflation over time.

As I mentioned earlier, how soon you start saving for retirement is very important. If you wait 10 or 15 years to begin saving for retirement, it's going to be a lot more difficult to accumulate the retirement savings that you would like in order to live in the way that you're accustomed to. As you may already know, the effects of compounding interest will allow your retirement savings to grow exponentially, rather than just linearly. Thus, after you've accumulated a decent amount of savings then the investment returns will continue to give you greater and greater increases right before you retire.

Obviously, how much you save has a big impact on your ideal retirement. If you only save a hundred dollars a month, you're never going to accumulate enough money to cover your standard of living in retirement that you have been used to. You need to be saving 10% of your income and possibly more in most cases.

One of the other biggest misconceptions is in estimating how much money you need during retirement. Inflation plays a huge role in how much money you are going to need to maintain your standard of living. In my own research I have noticed that a 1% change in inflation as a much bigger impact over the long haul versus a 1% increase in your investment return. I've seen retirement pictures look fine with a 2% inflation estimate, but "go all red" when you enter a 3% inflation estimate. "Going all red" is when you run out of money in retirement in the RetirementView program.

Another misconception I run into frequently is that "the government will take care of me". It is true that most Americans will receive Social Security benefits in retirement. But most people don't bother to find out how much they will be receiving from Social Security. In many cases, the amount you would receive from Social Security would barely get you over the poverty line in the

United States. So if you think Social Security is going to give you the easy life during retirement, you are sadly mistaken.

Social Security is just a slight supplement to your own retirement savings. In addition the Social Security fund is projected to go bankrupt sometime in the future because there will not be enough workers working to pay the benefits that will be required of all the retirees taking Social Security. The bottom line is that "the government may not take care of you." And even if the government gives you Social Security or other retirement related benefits, it will never give you the lifestyle you have been accustomed to without supplementing with your own retirement savings and investments.

What can you do to keep your money safe for retirement? Most people think that CDs and money markets are a great place to keep your retirement money. Is that a good idea?

Again I am not a financial advisor giving you advice. But I want you to think about CDs and money markets. What kind of return are they paying these days? Most CDs pay less than 1%. Inflation is running typically over 2% a year. We could at some point see inflation go back up to three and 4% a year. In either case, CDs and money markets are not even keeping up with inflation. That means the buying power of your savings is going down as the price of goods and services go up.

One thing you could consider is an annuity. There are many types of annuities. One type is called a fixed annuity. You agree to loan your money to the insurance company for a fixed period of time and in return they are going to guarantee a return on your investment. Often times this return is much higher than CDs or money markets.

When you talk about "safety", you are typically talking about avoiding losses in the stock market. Many investment managers use loss minimization strategies to try to illuminate or reduce any losses you might suffer in the event of a stock market crash. For example, trailing stop losses that are set on your investments can be triggered automatically when the stock market tanks to reduce the chances of your portfolio losing 20, 30, 40% of your portfolio.

If you have most of your retirement savings in mutual funds and stocks, you may want to find a financial advisor or investment manager that specializes in avoiding market losses. It may take some research to find those advisers, but they are out there.

What is one of the biggest pieces of advice you would give to anyone saving for retirement, or even to those who haven't even started saving for retirement?

My biggest piece of advice is that you need to know your numbers. You need to run some calculations that include everything that can possibly affect your retirement. This will include all of your investment accounts and their returns. This will include your Social Security and any pensions that you have. This will include your spouse if they're also saving for retirement. It will also include any other income items that could affect your retirement like life insurance, a part-time job, downsizing your home, rental property income, severance packages, selling a business, and any other income item that you can think of that may help your retirement.

As part of these calculations, you also need to estimate how much you'll be spending in retirement as well as the effect of inflation on those expenses. This is not an easy thing to do, but we have tried in our software to make it as simple as possible for you to at least do an estimate. We will talk more about this in the next chapter.

FOR A FREE TRIAL DOWNLOAD OF THE RETIREMENT VIEW SOFTWARE, YOU CAN VISIT THE WEBSITE FOR THIS BOOK AT:

www.YourRetirementMadeSimple.com

or, visit our Company website at:

www.torrid-tech.com

Chapter 2

*Tips on How to
"Make YOUR Retirement
Simple"*

Timothy J. Turner, JD

Planning your retirement finances is complicated because there are so many moving parts to your situation. There are "variables" that change over time like your investment returns, inflation, and how much money you need to spend just to name a few.

In order to "Keep It Simple", you really need a piece of software that can let you put in all of the factors affecting your retirement. The problem is that there are not many good programs out there. And of the ones that do exist, most of them are way too complicated.

What do I mean by that?

How can I tell if a software program is "too complicated"?

Here is a checklist of things you should look for when buying retirement or financial planning software:

1. **Is It easy to learn?** – It should not require you to travel to a multi-day training class. If it does, then it's "too darn complicated".

2. **Is It easy to use?** – if it takes 2 hours to put in a plan, then it's too complicated. You should be able to build a basic plan in as little as 10-15 minutes.

3. **Is It visual?** – the software should rely heavy on "visuals" to convey the plan. The visual should be meaningful and interesting. If your software is boring gray and full of columns of

numbers, then most people won't like it or understand it. Colors are good. An interesting screen that let's you visually see "your retirement picture" is the best.

4. Can you do Instant changes on the fly to see the impact on your plan? – if the software requires you to go back into your office, clear your afternoon schedule, and spend time alone poring over a manual to figure out how to make the plan, then you are lost before you begin. A great tool should be able to let you quickly change the factors and INSTANTLY see the effect on the plan, right on the screen in front of your eyes.

5. How long is the printed report? - The printed report given to the client should be about 10 pages at most. If you go longer than that, then you will confuse and bore your client. So if your software prints out 50, 80, 100, 150 page reports, then you are probably making a big mistake. (*Seriously some advisors are doing that*)

6. Does it work on Windows AND Mac computers? – you are probably committed to one platform or the other right now, but think about the future and whether you ever want to switch. Having software that runs on BOTH platforms, as a native application, is important because it gives you the most flexibility and options in the future.

7. **Where is your data stored and is it secure?** – a lot of software programs are "in the cloud" and on the internet. As such, your data is also out on the internet, ready for the next hacker that figures out how to hack into that system. Are you really sure that info is safe? When you store the client data locally on your own computers, then you don't need to worry about "hackers" stealing your client data. The peace of mind knowing your customer's data is safe will help you to rest easy every night of the week, including weekends and holidays!

Why can't I just use some of the free calculators that I see on the Internet?

People bring this up to me all the time. There are a lot of free calculators out there on the Internet. Some of them come from big fortune 500 companies. There are some that even our company Torrid Technologies has licensed to other companies. But most of these programs have a number of deficiencies that make them way less than ideal for planning your retirement.

For one thing, most of these calculators are not private. The big company may be monitoring what you're putting into the systems and then using it in their marketing. Another issue is that sometimes the calculations are skewed with assumptions that favor the products or services that the company is offering. So in other words, the calculators are not unbiased .

Another issue is that most of the calculators you'll find online do not take into account the spouse. Which means you can't look at a complete picture of what your retirement might look like because you're not including your spouse's retirement plan and their Social Security and any other information related to what your spouse brings to the table. This leads to a really inaccurate projection and is pretty much useless.

In addition, most of the free calculators that are out on the Internet do not properly handle taxes. They just don't go into the detailed level of taxation that a retirement calculation really needs to go into to be accurate. it's crucial that taxes are accounted for not only during the time that you're saving, but also during retirement when you are going to be taking withdrawals out of all the different retirement accounts that you have. Without accounting for the taxation, your income ability in retirement could be off by 20 or 30% or more.

Another issue is security. How secure are these calculators online? Is somebody going to have access to your information? Many of the calculators don't store the data which is great for security. But it's not so great for you because you have to re-enter the data every time you want to revisit your retirement plan.

There's another algorithm required when doing retirement calculations called the Required Minimum Distributions. This is where the U.S. federal government requires you to make distributions from your qualified retirement accounts once you reach age 70 1/2. Why did they do that? Because they want to start getting some tax money. And even though it's not a complicated calculation, it is something that's important in an overall retirement calculation and that most online calculators don't account for.

Another area that online financial calculators are weak in is in creating a Social Security estimate. Now you can go to the SSA.gov website and use one of their calculators to generate an estimate. But most of the retirement calculators that are on mutual fund company websites don't necessarily include a Social Security estimate. They asked for you to enter your own estimate. And maybe you don't know what you're going to get from your Social Security benefits. In addition even if they do include it, they don't properly calculate taxes on Social Security which is a complicated calculation. Part of your Social Security is not taxable. But part of it can be 50 or 85% taxable. It's important to take this into account into any retirement estimate that you might do.

So if you decide to use a free online calculator for your retirement planning, know that it probably is not accurate in many ways and will in the long run cause you to lose time in making adjustments that could correct possible shortfalls in retirement.

Can you tell us at a high level about Torrid Tech's RetirementView program? What is it and why do people use it?

RetirementView is our software program that runs on Mac or Windows computers, or soon on the cloud (without the limitations of other calculators that are on the internet).   It's designed to be really easy to use. And what I mean by that is that if you can fire up the program and fill in the blanks that we have provided for you, then you can build your own retirement picture. It's something that anyone of any age can do.

The benefit is that you get to see visually whether you're going to run out of money or not. Retirement View shows you in red when you're going to be in trouble, and you can just roll your mouse over the picture to see what age you're going to have an issue.

One of the big advantages of the software is that it's under your control. So it's more private and secure than anything that you could do from a free calculator online, and we are an unbiased source since we don't sell any financial products or services. We don't try to slant the calculations to favor any one particular financial product or service.

In addition, since you have the software and all of your inputs at your fingertips, you can make changes to your plan at any time. You don't have to run to your financial advisor every single time you're thinking about changing something, or even every time you get your investment statements.

Who should be using the RetirementView software?

The software is good for anyone that wants to figure out their retirement finances whether you're still working and saving for retirement or already retired and trying to watch your nest egg. It works for people of all ages even Millennial's and even those that are quite up there in age in their 80s and 90s.

If you were still working that is the best time to make adjustments to the amount that you're saving as well as where you're putting your savings to maximize the amount you'll have at retirement. RetirementView will help you estimate how much you can accumulate for retirement. It will help you make decisions about what age you can retire.

If you are already retired, you need to watch your investments and expenses carefully. You need to find a balance between your spending and your income streams, as well as the growth on your investments. And you need to be able to do all this in the context of inflation and taxes. This is quite a complicated task but the RetirementView program makes it simple as pie for you to figure out.

How is it possible for someone with no financial planning experience or background to build their own retirement plan picture?

That's a great question. Mainly we've studied retirement planning for over 24 years and we've put that expertise into the software. We thought about just about anything that you might want to enter into the program. And we figured out how to let you do that quickly and easily.

In addition, the engine that runs the calculations does a lot of the complicated things for you behind the scenes so that you don't even have to think about ithem. For example, it calculates your Required Minimum Distributions on qualified plans. It calculates taxes on Social Security using the same algorithm the IRS explains on its website. It takes into account inflation. It takes into account that you might have a spouse and that you are both targeting a retirement life together.

It accounts for a lot of things that you may not have even thought about or don't even know about. It will take you years to learn about all the different topics that we have embedded into the program automatically.

So again if you can turn on your computer, install the software, and fill in the blanks, then the program will run the calculations for you and show you whether you are going to run out of money. You can then make changes to your plan quickly and easily to see immediately what the effect on your plan will be from those changes.

How do we know we can trust the output from your program?

We have been working on the software program since 1993. So that's a long time for a software program. During that time we've had fortune 500 companies review the program, as well as actuarial firms and thousands of financial advisors. When we have found any problem or a bug, then we have fixed it as promptly as we can.

So the biggest reason why you can trust the output of the program is that true professional financial advisors use our software in their practices with their clients. They wouldn't be doing that if they didn't trust the output from the program.

Note that the financial industry is heavily regulated. There are a lot of rules, laws, and regulations that dictate how financial advisors and financial companies operate. If there was a substantial problem with the output from the software, then it certainly would've been found by now. All that being said even if we find an issue, we feel it is our job as a company to correct any problems that

36

might arise. Our job is to offer the highest quality retirement planning software that we possibly can. And that is one of the reasons that so many customers continue to use our software year after year.

What types of income items does the RetirementView system cover?

It can cover any income item that you can think of, whether that income item is a one-time lump sum or income that comes in over a number of years. We call these type of income items "Cash Infusions" and created a special screen to include them.

Here is a short list of examples:

- selling your home

- downsizing your home

- rental properties

- part-time job in retirement

- life insurance proceeds

- inheritances

- retirement packages

- severance packages

- sale of a business

- partnership earnout

- reverse mortgages

Let's go into detail about many of these items, so you can understand better how RetirementView can provide a comprehensive retirement picture even though it is so simple and easy to use.

DOWNSIZING YOUR HOME

Let's take the example of "downsizing your home" in retirement. You raised 4 kids and have a big 4 bedroom house. It's too big and has too much upkeep and a big yard. You want to move to a much smaller condo and save on utilities, taxes, and insurance. By doing so, you can also pull out equity that you can use for your retirement.

So let's pretend you are retiring at age 66 and at that time you will sell your home one year later and move to a condo. That one year will give you the time to clean out all those closets, the garage, and the attic and get rid of all the junk you don't need. Let's say that your house sells for $430,000 (obviously this is just a hypothetical example) and the real estate commission takes the $30,000. This leaves you with $400,000 to buy a condo.

But wait, you don't want to buy a $400,000 condo because you are downsizing and want to take out some equity. So you shop around for a $200,000 condo and find one that suits your needs. Voila! You just injected a "Cash Infusion" of $200,000 into your retirement nest egg. This could really help you in retirement.

Of course, there are other considerations that may prevent you from doing this. Maybe you just can't bear to leave the house you raised your kids in. Maybe you love your neighborhood, your neighbors and don't want to leave your "support netwok". Obviously, with the software we are just calculating the numerical factors, not the emotional ones.

In the RetirementView program, you would click on "Cash Infusions". Select any line and enter the description "Downsize our home" and value of $200,000. You would enter the Start Age for this to be 67 - the age you plan to sell your home and downsize. You would enter a Duration of 1 because this is a one-time event. Most likely you will not owe any taxes on the gain, but you would need to consult your CPA about that. If you do owe taxes on the gain, then you can enter that tax rate as well right on the Cash Infusion line.

That's it. You then look at your ongoing investments to see that they have shot up. You then check your "retirement picture" - the Retirement Income Graph - and see immediately that "some of the red is now gone". You can roll your mouse over it to see the new age that you run out of money (or not).

By adding these types of things into your plan, you can hopefully improve your retirement picture and outlook. You can add or change these items to "experiment" and play "what if" with different options that you want to consider.

RENTAL PROPERTIES

Let's say you own 2 rental properties and you want to account for them in your retirement picture. Again you would enter them as a "Cash Infusion". You would end up using one line for each rental property - that would be 2 lines for 2 properties.

First, you want to model your rental income from the properties. Clicking on Cash Infusions you would enter the first property on any line that you choose. I would enter something like "Rent 123 Main Street" as the description and then enter the net rent. If it were $1,000 a month, then enter $12,000 as the annual amount. Set the Start age to when you start retirement, unless you are SAVING all of that money prior to retirement and not spending it. The duration would be how long you will collect the rents until you sell the property.

If you plan to keep the property until the end, then enter a big number for the duration like 40 years. But if you plan to sell the property, for example, at age 72 when you don't want to be messing with it anymore, then enter duration 6 (assuming you retire at 66).

You would then use another line to enter the rent from your second property.

What about selling the property?

Well, let's say we sell property 1 at age 72 as we mentioned above. I would use a 3rd line to model "Sell 123 Main Street" and enter the value of the property. For this example, let's say the property is worth $250,000 and has no mortgage. I would enter the value $250,000. If it were growing in value, I would enter a growth rate on the Cash Infusion line. We would then enter age 72 for the age to start the infusion and duration of "one" since it is a one-time lump sum.

You would enter a similar line for your second property. In this way, you can model the "rental income" and the "income from the sale of the property" for an unlimited number of properties. We have seen this to be a valuable tool for landlords who are planning their retirement years.

A more complicated way to model the above scenario is to enter gross numbers for the rent and sale of property, and then enter "Special Expenses" for things like taxes, insurance, utilities, and real estate agent fees. In this way you can estimate the income items and the expenses separately for more detailed tracking.

PART-TIME JOB

Many people think that they can just work part-time in retirement to make ends meet. This is a great way to stay active and provide extra income that will make your investment accounts last longer. However, keep in mind that this all depends on your health. If you are not

41

healthy enough to work, then you will not be able to work part-time.

For now, let's assume you are healthy enough to work part-time. Your last employer hates to see you retire. You have so much knowledge and experience. They beg you to work 15 hours a week, even if it's just to be around to answer questions related to your accounts and your projects. They agree to pay you just $25,000 for this part-time work, but that includes 8 weeks of vacation for you to take plenty of time off.

In the RetirementView program, you would go to Cash Infusions again and click on any line. Enter for the description "Part-time job" and then enter $25,000 for the annual value. Let's put that it starts at age 66 and the duration will be 5, assuming you work there for another 5 years part-time. For taxes, you will enter your ordinary effective tax rate. Let's assume it's 20%. Add that into your plan and see how this idea will affect your retirement picture. It should make your investments last a little longer as it reduces the burn rate early in your retirement.

LIFE INSURANCE PROCEEDS

You are smart and have a life insurance policy. The purpose is to provide for your spouse when you pass away. The face value of the policy is $500,000. How would this be included in your retirement plans?

Well, again you would go to the Cash Infusions screen and use any line to enter "Life insurance proceeds" and then enter the value of $500,000. But at what age will you set it to occur? That's a little tricky because obviously that is when you are guessing that you pass away, which really only God knows.

But at least you can put in a few different ages to see how this life insurance will affect your retirement plan and also the plans of your spouse. Duration would be "one" since it would be a one-time payment from the insurance company. The tax rate would be zero in most cases.

I have looked at a lot of retirement plans and in many cases the retirement picture looks a bit shaky. I see cases where there is a spouse 5, 10 or even 15 years or more younger than the other. The life insurance proceeds coming into the picture typically helps the situation dramatically for the surviving spouse. You can see it right there on the screen.

As before you may not know "when" this money will come into the picture, but once you see the effect you will be sure to keep up with those premiums.

INHERITANCES

Like the life insurance, no one knows much about their inheritance, or even if there is one. And for those that are aware of a possible inheritance, they certainly don't know "when" it will happen.

So it's pretty speculative.

However, you can enter it on Cash Infusions just to "see" how that would affect your retirement at various ages. I wouldn't put a lot of dependence on it, but at least you can consider the effect of it on your retirement picture, and do so quickly and easily.

RETIREMENT AND SEVERANCE PACKAGES

You are close to retirement, but not yet there. Perhaps you are 62 years old. Your employer wants to cut 10% of its workforce to save on expenses. They offer a voluntary severance package to anyone that wants to take it. How do you know if it's a good deal or not?

Without running a few calculations, you just won't know.

My suggestion to you would be to run one plan that assumes you work until the age you plan to work. This will continue your ongoing retirement plan contributions, but more importantly not start the spenddown of your accounts until later. So first, work on that "retirement picture" first.

Then, make some changes to account for this "package" they are offering you. First, change your retirement age to now age 62, assuming you won't find another job, but are considering retiring early. This WILL begin the spenddown of your accounts in our program.

Second, go to the Cash Infusions screen and use any line for "severance package" then enter the amount. If it's a one-time severance amount, enter the full value and duration of "one". If they will pay you the severance over time, then enter the number of years of the payout. So if they say they will pay you $120,000 over 3 years, you would enter annual value $120,000 and a duration of 3 for three years.

Does this make sense?

In this way, you can compare "continuing to work" to the "severance package" to see which one appears to be the better deal.

Now you might conclude that "working longer" is the better deal. But keep in mind that many companies start with "voluntary" severance and when they don't hit their targets they move on to "involuntary" severance (i.e. layoffs). Take that into consideration when making your decision. If you turn down the voluntary package, what are the chances you can keep your job through the age that you really want to retire?

SALE OF A BUSINESS

Perhaps you own your own business, or prac- tice. Maybe you are a dentist or lawyer. Regardless of when you retire, you might sell your business or partnership interest to someone else. And when you do, you want to model what that looks like and how that will affect the future of your retirement.

Even if it's some big number, you want to look at how that affects all of your retirement plans, even if that includes buying that lake house you always wanted, or doing some serious travel around the world.

Again you are going to use the Cash Infusions screen and use any line for the sale of your business. If it is a one-time lumpsum buyout, enter the enter value and a duration of "one". The Start Age would be the age you sell the business whether that is your retirement age or not.

Do you owe taxes on the transaction and if so how much? You will have to consult your CPA on that one because it depends on too many factors. But rest assured whatever they say you can enter into the RetirementView to see how it will affect your picture.

If the sale is an earnout or paid over multiple years, you simply enter the annual payout and set the duration to the number of years. If the payouts are different, then use one line for each year and enter the exact payout schedule. In this way you can model just about any method that the deal is structured and still see how it will affect your specific retirement picture.

If you do end up buying that lake house, enter that as a Special Expense! And then enjoy all the fishing and boating that you are looking forward to....

What about the "expense" side of retirement? How can we manage that so that we don't get out of balance?

Retirement is truly a "balancing act". On the one hand you have your investments, possibly some interest or returns, and some income streams. On the other hand, you have your expenses, all of the foreseen and UNFORESEEN expenses that you have to deal with in retirement.

We have already talked about a number of difference income streams, so now let's talk about the "expense side".

In light of our "Keep It Simple" approach, the dirt simplest way to model your expenses is just with a reasonable estimate of annual expenses, plus add an inflation factor. In RetirementView we would just enter a "Retirement Income Goal" and "Inflation". The program would then use that to project out your picture and figure out how you are going to pay for all of those expenses. I would call this the "thumbnail" approach.

How do you know what to enter?

Many people including advisors tell you to enter 70 - 80% of your pay from your last year of work. So if you made $100,000 enter $80,000. I find this pretty simplistic. If you really know that you always stick to an annual budget, then maybe it will work for you.

Another option is to create a "budget" where you list every single thing you are going to spend money on in retirement, and eliminate the things you won't be spending money on like work clothes and commuting to work. This can take a long time, but you can do this and enter every single item on our "Special Expenses" worksheet. We have seen many people do this. The disadvantage is that it is time intensive compared to the rest of the program.

Ultimately, you may really have to create a budget to try to accurately reflect your retirement. Perhaps you use a budgeting software program. There are many out there of course. If you are already tracking your budget just transfer those numbers over into RetirementView.

Some people already have a budget in Microsoft Excel. Same thing. Just transfer the totals over into RetirementView.

What if you want to model retirement in "periods"?

For example, you are going to travel and play golf a lot for the first 5 years, but after that slow down and eliminate big travel trips. In RetirementView, you could use multiple lines on "Special Expenses" to model different "periods" of expenses in retirement. For example, you could model your retirement in 3 periods using only 3 lines.

The first line you enter $80,000 as the annual value, starting at age 66, with a duration of 5 to cover the first five years. On another line, you reduce your expenses by $10,000 because you are eliminating travel. On that line you enter $70,000 a year starting at age 71 for a duration of 10 years. Then finally you use a third line to model the rest of your life. Perhaps you only need $60,000 at that point. You start that at age 81 and enter a duration of say 30 to run to the end of your retirement plan.

Using this method you can quickly and easily model as many retirement "periods" as you want.

What if you are married and want to model your retirement?

In our software we call this the "Couples" edition. In that version you can enter both of your relevant retirement information. The software has a tab of data for EACH OF YOU separately that covers your investments, your job income, your savings, your investment returns, your Social Security, and your Pensions (if you have one).

But the beauty of the system is that it combines all of that information into one common picture and runs calculations TOGETHER to see whether you can meet your common expense targets throughout retirement. Thus, the RetirementView program models reality in assessing a couples retirement future.

Each spouse's information is easily changeable at the click of a mouse. Just click on an item, edit it, and hit enter. That's it. The plan recalculates based on the changed input.

Both of you can sit there and "see" your retirement plan and how it's going to unfold.

The program can also estimate your Social Security if you don't know what it will be. Again, this creates an "estimate". Your best option is to go to SSA.gov and request an official estimate.

In most cases, one spouse is good with numbers and the other one is not. RetirementView is great in that case because the "numbers" spouse can enter all the dat,a but share the visual "results" with their spouse. ANYONE can understand that "red is bad" and "green is good". The program makes it easy for even non-technical and non-math oriented people to "discuss" their retirement picture.

After you have entered all of your information and are seeing "RED" all over your retirement, what are some high level things you can do to "improve" the picture and "get the red out"?

This is really the fun part of retirement planning - playing around with the factors to see "how" you can eliminate the shortfalls in your retirement picture. We call this game "get the red out". You will keep editing factors until you can "get the red out".

Now remember when we said that starting early and doing planning as an ongoing exercise is really important? This is where the rubber meets the road. If you have waited too late, then your options will be very limited.

Let's start with someone who is still working and some of the factors they can adjust to improve their retirement.

There are 5 big changes you can make to "get the red out":

1). save more money in your working years

2). find a way to get better investment returns on your retirement savings

3). retire later

4). reduce your spending in retirement more than you wanted to

5). move to a state with lower tax rates

These are the big five and some of them you frankly aren't going to like.

1). Save More Money

Sure these changes are obvious. But how do you know how much more to save? If you have entered all your info into RetirementView, you can just keep increasing your savings until you "get the red out".

Now note that your contributions to some retirement plans are "limited" by IRS laws. For example, in 2017 if you are under 50 you can save a maximum of $18,000 into a 401(k) plan or traditional IRA. IF you are 50 or over, you can save an additional $6,500 for a total of $24,500. (Source: IRS.gov)

Maybe you can't save any more right now. Maybe you can. Regardless you can run some numbers to see how much this will affect your retirement picture.

2). Get Better Investment Returns

Again, I am not giving you "financial advice" as to where to put your investments or what stocks to buy. I'm just pointing out the reality of the "Rule of 72" which is that if you divide your investment return into 72, it will tell you how many years it will take to double your investment account balance. Thus, if you get a 4% average return then it will take you 18 years to double your investment account (not including additional savings). If you get a 5% average return it will take you 14.4 years.

This is the value of compounding. The higher the return obviously the faster your accounts will compound.

I am not advocating what amount of risk you should or should not take. I'm only pointing out that as your investment returns go up, then the more likely you can provide for your standard of living in retirement, from a MATHMATICAL RETURN STANDPOINT - not from a risk standpoint.

Generally, you are taking on more "risk" when you try to get better investment returns. This is where you should find a good investment manager or financial advisor that can manage your portfolio for you. They can analyze your risk tolerance and find an investment mix that is right for you.

3). Retire Later

OK I'm sure you didn't want to hear this one. You've been waiting more than 30 or 40 years to finally retire, and the last thing you want to hear is "you need to work a few more years".

Unfortunately, reality may dictate that you do this or pay dearly later. If you run out of money at age 80, would you look back and say "gosh I should have worked a couple of more years". The average age of longevity is going up around the world mainly due to advances in medical science, physical fitness, and nutrition. We all know that.

From a retirement standpoint, if you delay retirement even 2 or 3 years, that will let you continue to save more money into your retirement accounts. It will also let you DELAY spending down your accounts, which has an even bigger effect on your retirement.

I know you may not want to do it, but try testing working a little longer just to see what kind of effect it has on your retirement picture.

4). Reduce Retirement Spending

Again this one is obvious, but how do you know how much you have to reduce spending? In RetirementView, if you entered a Retirement Income Goal of say $80,000 a year and you are running out of money, change it to $75,000 and see how much longer your investments last. Then try $70,000. Maybe $65,000. Just to see how it changes your overall picture. Maybe you can't reduce your spending that much. Or perhaps if you saw how much it helps your situation, you might be incentivized to figure out how you can reduce your burn rate.

5). Move to a State with Lower Tax Rates

Obviously, this is not for everyone. Many people do relocate to the states that have no income tax. But be careful because some of those states have other taxes that are higher like real estate. Use the internet to re-search the tax favorability of the state you are consider-ing.

In the RetirementView software, you can just change the state tax rate in retirement to zero if your new state has no income tax. If they have higher real estate taxes, perhaps you enter a Special Expense for the added amount and turn that on and off as you compare scenarios.

You will need to account for moving costs as well. There are a number of considerations including where your family is located and what health care you need. Some people are considering moves overseas to places that have a much reduced cost of living. Just remember that the ones who make that work from a financial point, typically complete the sale their residence here in the U.S. and move their entire life to these lower cost locations. If you want to be close to your kids and grandkids that might not be something you want to do.

Regardless, RetirementView lets you easily model these changes in both taxation and expenses so that you can see the effect on YOUR specific retirement situation.

THE GRAND-DADDY OF CHANGES TO GET THE RED OUT

Now that I've listed a few obvious changes you can make, I wanted to point out that the "Granddaddy" of all changes that has the biggest effect is to do a "combination" of these items!

It might not just be one thing. It is probably going to be several changes that you need to make in order to "get the red out" of your retirement picture.

For example, you have put everything you can think of into the RetirementView and it still says you run out of money at age 75. You are worried because you know your family tends to live well into their 80s and a few have cracked 90.

SO you start trying combinations. What if you try the following:

- increase your savings from 10% of your pay to 12% of your pay

- move your retirement back 2 years and also have your spouse do the same

- reduce expenses in retirement by 10%

- move to a tax free state

NOW look at your picture. You should see it change for sure. Now perhaps your investments last until age 81. If that's not good enough, then keep going. Try even more changes. Retire 4 years later and increase your savings to 14%.

This is just a hypothetical example, but it is designed to show you some basic techniques that should help with your retirement picture in "getting the red out".

What about medical issues, assisted living, and related nursing care as a part of retirement planning?

This one is a BIG issue. More people are living longer but not able to care for themselves. They just can't live alone anymore and family members are not equipped to provide the care they need.

The costs of care can be high. You can research on the internet the cost in your area of the different types of care.

In the RetirementView program, you would model these costs under "Special Expenses". You can enter the annual amount and estimate a duration that you will pay them, even if it's to the end of the plan (which can be expensive).

My grandmother had Alzheimer's and lived for over 10 years in a nursing home facility. That's a long time to be paying for care and is quite expensive. Most people think the government will pay for all of that, but only if you have spent down almost all of your savings. "Medicaid planning" is an entirely separate topic that we don't cover in this book, but is worth looking into.

To wrap up, why is "planning" so important these days?

As the old saying goes, "if you fail to plan, then you are planning to fail". Did you know that most people spend more time planning their annual vacation then they do planning for their retirement? Your vacation might last one or two weeks, while your retirement could last 30 or 40 years!

As I write this, my wife's grandmother is 101 years old and lives in an assisted living facility in Alabama. It has taken a lot of planning and preparation to get her the care that she needs. What are you going to do if you live to be 101? Will your retirement finances be able to withstand that longevity?

My hope for you is that you will do the planning needed, so that you can have the peace of mind to enjoy your retirement and be a blessing to other people, instead of a burden.

Can you tell us about what computers your software runs on, as well as how someone can try it out?

Sure. The RetirementView program is mainly designed to run on Windows(r) and Mac(r) computers. This includes Windows(r) tablets. We now have a cloud version if you want to run it on an Apple(r) iPad though. So it can run on desktops, laptops, Macbooks, you name it.

Our goal is to let you use it on any device that you want to use it on.

FOR A FREE TRIAL DOWNLOAD OF THE RETIREMENT VIEW SOFTWARE, YOU CAN VISIT THE WEBSITE FOR THIS BOOK AT:

www.YourRetirementMadeSimple.com

or, visit our Company website at:

www.torrid-tech.com

You can also call us at 1-888-333-5095 and request a demo CD to be mailed to you. Tell them you saw this offer in my book.

As founder of Torrid Technologies since 1993, Tim Turner has designed numerous financial planning software programs including Retirement View for Windows and Mac, WebCalcs(r), WebCalcs(r) for Advisors, as well as numerous custom planning systems. Thousands of consumers have used Retirement View to quickly and easily build a visual retirement picture that they can instantly make changes to and see how their retirement might play out.

Tim has taught thousands of financial advisors and insurance agents how to use his strategies and system to dramatically improve their financial practice and their incomes. His RetirementView system is used by financial advisors and reps at major Broker/Dealers like LPL, National Planning Corp, NEXT, OneAmerica, Commonwealth Financial, and Lincoln Financial. Tim's WebCalcs(r) software systems have also been used by millions of people on websites for Pacific Life, AXA, The Hartford, TIAA-

CREF, JANUS, MFS, The MONY Group, MassMutual, and Sun Life.

FINANCIAL ADVISOR
calls RetirementView "Easy-to-Use"   and   "surprisingly good for basic planning".

LIFE INSURANCE SELLING calls it "a simple and easy way (the best I've seen) to create a customer scenario in only 10 minutes".

RETIREMENT INCOME JOURNAL says this system "is worth a look... If you want something quick, simple to use, and easy for clients to understand."

Tim graduated from Boston University as a Trustee Scholar with a B.S. in Electrical Engineering, Summa Cum Laude, and from NCCU Law School, Magna Cum Laude. He is also an attorney and member of the Georgia Bar. He is married with 4 kids and lives outside of Atlanta, Georgia.

CONTACT INFORMATION
Phone: 1.888.333.5095
Email: tturner@torrid-tech.com
Website: http://www.torrid-tech.com
Facebook: https://www.facebook.com/torridtech/
Linkedin: https://www.linkedin.com/in/tim-turner-b89ba83
You Tube:
https://www.youtube.com/user/TorridTechnologies

Chapter 3

Life is More Than a Paycheck

by Chuck Price, CRFA, CSA

"Be more concerned with your character than your reputation, because your character is what you really are, while your reputation is merely what others think of you."

-John Wooden

Tim Turner: Okay, this is Tim Turner and I'm here with Chuck Price today. He's been in the financial services business since 1970 and he helps pre-retirees and those already retired to develop and follow a strategy to prevent them from running out of money in retirement. Today he's president of Price Financial Group Wealth Management, Inc. out of Portland, Oregon and he has the longest running live radio show in American that features a financial advisor, an estate planning attorney and a CPA answering live questions on the air. His radio show is live on four different stations simultaneously in the Portland area and it's also aired in Phoenix and it's called Investing Simplified. Chuck, are you there?

Chuck Price: Yes I am.

All right, great. So glad to have you on today.

Chuck Price: Thanks Tim.

All right, so can you start by just sharing a little bit about yourself, maybe your family and where you grew

up and what your hobbies are. What do you like to do in your spare time? That sort of thing.

Chuck Price: Sure, absolutely. I'm married and we have four children. I grew up in Vancouver, Washington which is right across the river from Portland, Oregon. Not to be confused with Vancouver, BC, but Vancouver USA. I grew up basically on a farm, working on a farm, and as a young person I knew I wanted to do something besides work on a farm for the rest of my life. That's how I gravitated into getting into the financial services. I also spent six years in the US Marine Corps Reserves, and learned a lot of valuable lessons being in the Marine Corp during the Vietnam area. That was very, very helpful to me in my life as far as setting goals and achieving things. You learn some very basic fundamentals about achieving things that you think you couldn't achieve but you actually find out you can!

Wow.

Chuck Price: My wife and I have grown up in the Vancouver area. We've not moved more than nine miles our entire life and still live in that community.

Well that's great. I hear also you're big into golf.

Chuck Price: Yes, I try to play golf as much as I can and I'm one of those really lucky people because my wife is addicted to golf. Since we both love to play golf, we do our vacations around golf and we spend a lot of time golfing. Mark Twain had a famous saying, "Golf is the ruination of a good walk in the park" My wife and I have the total different opinion, . We can walk and play golf and we cannot play the whole round without laughing or finding something very funny about which one of us did, that messed up a shot or did something. We find it as great therapy as a husband and wife to go out there and be together, and sometimes we don't even keep score.

I guess everybody wants to know, has she beaten you?

Chuck Price: Yes, she has. Once.

Once?

Chuck Price: One day she beat me. We were playing a par three and she beat me good. Yes, she did.

Well, that's fun. That's good to hear.

Chuck Price: Yes. Something I will never forget, it keeps me humble.

All right, so let's change gears a little bit. Can you tell us a story maybe about your childhood that had a big impact on your life?

Chuck Price: I think one of the biggest impacts on my life is when I was a kid because living on a farm we didn't have a lot of luxuries and stuff. I had an uncle on my mother's side who was a very successful life insurance agent with MetLife. He was like my mother's rich uncle and we went to his place. I had never seen such a beautiful place. I was probably 10 or 11 years old and at that point in my life my dream was to be a pro baseball player because I loved baseball. I still love baseball to this day. In fact, my wife and I try to go down to Phoenix to spring training for the Mariners every year. I love baseball. We go up to the Mariner games as well or we watch all the Mariner games at home on DirectTV.

But I saw how his living, his lifestyle was and I knew at that age that that was how I wanted to live. I wanted to live in a different lifestyle than I was growing up in. That's not to say anything about my parents because we had 26 acres and we had a great community. My neighbors are still my friends to this day that I grew up with. We all bailed hay together, we all grew vegetables together, and hunted together. We did all that kind of stuff. Those are roots that you can never break. They're a good foundation and hard work never hurt anybody. I really value the fact that I got to grow up like that because I learned the value of hard work.

That's great. You're right, most people don't necessarily learn the value of hard work and you're starting to see that today.

Chuck Price: That's sad, but true!

Let's switch gears and talk about the financial business. How did you get into the financial business? What attracted you to it? Just how you got started.

Chuck Price: Well, after school and while serving my six months of active duty in the Marine Corps Reserves, I was working at a restaurant as a restaurant manager trainee, which is really a glorified busboy, and I was there when my first son was born and a guy came along to try to get me to buy life insurance, which I knew I needed to have more life insurance now that I had a child and responsibility. But I wasn't making enough money and he said, "Well, You're a bright young guy, why don't you come over and talk to us?"

I went over and talked to them and they offered me a job and I went to work for the Prudential insurance company and it was probably the greatest move I ever made because I doubled my income the first year and I was able to buy the life insurance. It just totally changed my life because it put me into an area that I knew very little about but realized very quickly that I had an aptitude for it and I loved it. I always remember my dad telling me, and I know it's not his saying, but my dad always told me, "Listen, if you can find a way to get paid for something you love to do, then you never work hard a day because you're doing what you love to do." I thought, "Man, I've found this because I love doing this and I get paid to help people", which is a pretty cool deal.

Yeah, that's great. Yeah, do what you love and you'll never work hard a day in your life.

Chuck Price: Yes, absolutely.

So you started at Prudential and I know where you are today. Just a brief summary of how you got from the first job at Prudential to where you are today.

Chuck Price: Well, when I was at Prudential for about eight years, like a lot of Insurance Companies at that point in time were going into securities investing as well. With Prudential I went and got my securities license and all of a sudden I discovered a whole world of opportunity that I never had just with a life insurance company where you had insurance and annuities but you didn't have the securities and the investment side. I got to learn that part of the business and it was a great eye-opener to me when I started looking at the investment world of the opportunities.

Then I ended up leaving Prudential and setting up my own general agency. I was doing securities and life insurance. At that point in time primarily doing mutual funds and limited partnerships and things like that. Then I ended up getting into the banking industry because one of my clients actually was the president of a bank. He ended up saying, "Hey, why don't you do this for all my customers?", and so he brought me in to the bank side of it. Through that we developed a business inside the Bank and in fact, a lot of clients I still have today I had at Prudential and I had when I started working through that bank system because those people are still my clients today. That was a long, long time ago. That opened my eyes to the banking world and the investment world, how they were merging together because it was changing times. Of course today it's way different than it was back then. But through that I ended up eventually going out on my own, setting up my own operation and being totally independent.

Probably the greatest thing I can say about independence is banks keep getting taken over and I went through several takeovers where people came in and took over the bank and we ended up working for somebody else and I realized that's not the kind of life I want to live. Besides that, I don't want some person telling me what to sell my clients or what to offer my clients. I want to do what's best for my client, not what somebody's telling me I got to offer. So I gravitated into going totally independent and becoming a registered investment advisor Firm so that I could work with my clients on a fiduciary responsibility basis where I became a fiduciary to offer what was best for my client, not what some bank or some insurance company or some investment firm was telling me to do, but what was best for my client!

That's great. Yeah, staying independent and recommending what they need rather than what some big company is telling you. I think that's what clients want to see these days.

Chuck Price: Yes, when I was with one of the banks and one of the reasons I left is because they wanted us to sell their crappy mutual funds, and in all honesty I told my supervisor at the time, I said, "I'm not going to sell this because I wouldn't buy them myself." He said, "Well, you don't have a choice." I said, "Oh, I always have a choice." My choice was to leave and that's what I did, I left. The bankers always think they control the client and they always go by the Golden Rule, them that got the gold rule, and they think they got all the money! The reality is, the customers are usually better off going through an independent person than somebody who's a captive person who is told what they can sell and when they sell it.

And when a big company says, "Jump!", and they have to say, "How high?"

Chuck Price: That's correct! The sad part about it is I still run into Advisors all the time and they have to sell what they're selling because that's all they have to offer. I feel bad for them. I've called some of them and I've got some to change because I ask them, "Why are you doing that? How do you sleep at night?"

Well, it took a lot of integrity for you to stick what you believe in, even if it meant leaving the bank. That says a lot about your personality and your character frankly.

Chuck Price: Yes, you have to take a leap of faith. If you believe that you're doing what's right, then you have to have the fortitude to have the faith to step forward and go out there and do the right thing for your client.

That's great. Let's talk about radio. How did you get into radio?

Chuck Price: Well, very strange story. A buddy of mine that I'd known for years and years lives in Boston, Massachusetts and he called me one day, because their radio show had got picked up on satellite with a Portland, Oregon radio station. They were here Monday through Friday in the morning, 7:00-9:00, doing a live talk show. They were starting to get a lot of leads in the Portland area and he didn't know anybody in Portland but me so he called me. He said, "Hey, you ever think about doing radio?" I said, "I don't know." He says, "Well, why don't you come on our show Tuesdays and Thursdays and we'll do a segment called Coast to Coast. You can talk about Portland and we'll talk about Boston and we'll see what's going on in the economies." I said, "Well, let's do it."

I did that for about three months and they got canceled and the local radio station that we were running on a satellite, the station manager called me and he said, "I've been listing to your part on Tuesdays." He said, "You really ought to come in and do your own radio show." I had never thought about it at the time and so I set up an appointment to meet with him but I went and called my attorney who'd been my attorney for about 10 years. He's an estate planning attorney that I worked with closely. He's my personal attorney. I said, "Let's you and I do a radio show together."

We started doing the radio show and I got to tell you it's been very, very successful. About a year later we added our CPA and now we have the longest running show in America that's a live radio show with a financial advisor, an estate planning attorney and a CPA. We answer questions Live on the air.

We also do a live podcast of the show. We've had people contact us from Atlanta, Georgia listening to our show on the web. We had a guy call from Missouri, a trucker who picks us up on the podcast, and listens to our show every Saturday. We're on Saturday live 8:00 AM Pacific Daylight Time and 11:00 AM on Eastern Daylight Time.

Now, what's the website if somebody wants to check out your radio show?

Chuck Price: They could listen to us at www.investingsimplifiedradio.com.

Okay, great. Let's talk about who is your ideal client? What types of people do you help?

Chuck Price: Probably the people I can help the most are people who are 50 and above. I wrote a book called "Investing Simplified" and I have Investing Simplified® as a registered trademark because I've designed a presentation about simple estate planning with Investing Simplified. The person we're looking for, as I mentioned in my book, you really need to start your planning 20 years ahead but the last 10 years of your retirement planning are critical.

We like to find people that are 10 years or less and get them on the right track to retirement because most people wait till they're retiring, about two or three years, and then they think, "Oh, you know what? Maybe we better do some planning." Well, it's a little late then. Then you're doing it by what you have the ability to do and it's really tough to change once you quit working. You're stuck in the pattern you're going to be in.

What we talk to people about is that last 10 years we want our clients to start living at least three to five years on 80% of the retirement income they're going to get when they retire. You can't believe the shock. People look at you and say, "Well, wait a minute. I'm still working. Why would I do that?" "Well, what happens if you got to retire today? What if you have a bad illness? If you're not used to living on that lower income, what's going to happen? You're going to spend all your savings. You're not going to have enough money to get to where you want to get to."

We think it's very important that people, always live below their means and get used to doing that because when you retire that is your means. That's it. Unless you're going to go get a job at Walmart and be a greeter or you're going to spend your golden years at the golden arches flipping burgers. You're going to want to have a retirement plan that will work and keep you out of that situation. I have a client that has a lot of money and he's a greeter at Walmart. He doesn't have to work but the only reason he's doing it is because he goes stir crazy being alone and he likes to do it because he talks to people and he's actually met some people there that have become friends of his because he didn't know a lot of people. I didn't have a problem with that if somebody wants to do that. The great thing is he can work when he wants to. That was built in to his retirement planning that he was going to probably work at some place like at Walmart just to meet people but not for an income.

Okay, so you started touching on how you help your ideal client. Talk more about that. What types of problems do you help them solve?

Chuck Price: Well, one of the things I try to tell my clients "Life is more than a paycheck".   If you spend your life all just living on your paycheck you're going to have a rude awakening when you retire because the paycheck you're going to get when you retire is not going to be as big as the one you're getting when you're working. Like I say, that to me is the thing that a lot of people have a tough time getting to because they procrastinate and wait till the day of reckoning, and then it's too late. I tell my clients, "You've got to start planning at least 10 years, and for sure five years before you retire.", because if you don't start living on that basis you're going to go through some very tough times. The idea of investing and saving your money is to enjoy retirement, not to have a stressful retirement.

I got to tell you Tim, my oldest client lived to be 103.

Wow.

Chuck Price: I just had a client that actually has been a client of mine actually since just about 1973. She turned 100 years old in December.

You know what she says to me, I meet with her three, four times a year, and she always says to me, "I had no idea I was going to have this much money when I got to be 100," because she never dreamed she'd live to be 100. But she is and she's doing just fine. She lives on her own. I've had numerous clients live to 100. The cool thing is not to run out of money.

That's phenomenal. Obviously when you live to be 100 you've probably been in retirement for more than 30 years so it's an amazing feat to live that long, but also not to run out of money. Also to keep your health up. My wife's grandmother is in great spirits and she hasn't run out of money but she does live in an assisted living facility because she has a number of health issues.

Chuck Price: Yes.

But she's going to be 101 this month.

Chuck Price: Wow, how cool is that?

Yeah.

Chuck Price: That is Great!

Yeah.

Chuck Price: Well, I wouldn't mind if I could have the ability to talk and take care of all my own stuff like this lady that's 100, I would be happy to do that. She's very, very lucky. She's stayed healthy and she can write her own checks still and pay all her own bills and lives by herself independently. I think that's great.

That's great. What a blessing.

Chuck Price: Yes, indeed.

Let's talk about some other things related to your practice. We've talked a little bit about some of the problems you help solve. What is the main thing that you want to help your ideal client with, besides just their retirement? What is your magic, expert ability, so to speak, and why do they want to become your client versus somebody else in your town?

Chuck Price: Well, I think one of the abilities that I have, and I've built my whole practice around Investing Simplified because I have the ability to take complex things and make them simplified. I think so many times people get so bogged down with complicated strategies that ends up confusing the situation and ends up confusing them and they end up doing nothing or whatever they do, they do poorly. I think that's one of the advantages we have in our office is we keep it simple. We don't make it complicated. We keep it simple and we always have an open line with our clients. Our clients always know they can reach me within any 24 hour period, except on the weekend obviously. But normally if they call our office they will have a callback within 24 hours and it'll either be me or one of my staff, but we will get back to them immediately because as we tell our clients, "There is no foolish question when it comes to your money or your investments."

That's really good. Tell me a little bit about what you do in the estate planning area. A lot of advisors don't ever touch that area and from talking to you before I know that's important to you.

Chuck Price: Well, the fortunate thing is my attorney, who is also a good friend, who I've been working with for well over 20 years and we do the radio show together, his office is right next door to mine. Him and I have probably done more estate planning seminars in the Portland area than any other financial planner and an estate planning lawyer. We've done a lot of seminars. But when we got into radio we discovered that we didn't have to go buy the dinners and do all the estate planning stuff, we could actually do it by just talking about different things. A lot of our show, Carl and I and Kevin, the CPA, the three of us talk about clients that we've worked with and we've helped solve their problems because having done it for all these years we have numerous clients, of course we never mention names, but we tell about different cases and different things that we were able to help clients do in their estate or Tax Planning. Of course the federal estate tax is up to five and a half million per person or eleven for a married couple, but Oregon has an estate tax starting at a million dollars. Well, if you have a 401k and a home, you've probably got a million dollars. A millionaire isn't what it was 20 years ago. It's a lot different today.

Yeah.

Chuck Price: A lot of people have an estate tax problem and they just have no clue that they have one. It is a big part of our business, absolutely.

Great. I was going to ask you, what are one or two popular misconceptions about the services that you provide for your clients, and/or the results related to what you do?

Chuck Price: What are misconceptions? Well, I think the biggest misconception that all advisors are the same or that you can go and walk into your bank and get the same advice you can get from talking to an independent advisor. It is totally night and day difference! I think that's the biggest thing that people don't understand. You really have the investment world broken into two areas. You have, one, the captive advisor that works for a bank or a large company like Bank America or Merrill Lynch or a big brokerage firm. They are limited to offer the products and services that their broker dealer or their bank offers and tells them to sell. This is what they're obligated to offer. In fact, if they sell away from the recommendation they can be terminated. Well, on the other hand, you've got registered investment advisor firms like mine where we actually have a fiduciary responsibility to our client. We go out and look at different products and services that other people wouldn't probably do, because we represent our clients and we have a Fiduciary Responsibility to what's in the best interest for our client. That is a big difference.

The other thing is many of them have deals with companies, mutual fund companies or insurance companies, where they get special incentives to sell products and services. Well, we don't do any of that because we're independent. We don't take any special concessions to offer any product and service. In fact, I get people calling me all the time wanting me to offer their products and giving me extra benefits to do them and I just tell them, "Look, that's not in the best interest of my client." You're going to pay me extra money to push a product. If your product's better I'll offer it, if it's not better I'm not offering it, I don't care what the incentive is and I think that's the big difference that people don't understand in our industry. Of course when we get to sit down with them we explain that to them.

Again, it goes back to your integrity and the way you strongly believe in doing what's right for the client versus just what lines your own pocket, and I think that's a big differentiator in what you're doing and a lot of other people in the industry that I've run into over the years.

Chuck Price: No, you're exactly correct.

Okay, so let's talk, you're on the radio or you get referrals and you're potentially meeting with new clients, people that are interested in maybe working with you. Can you describe the type of process that you take them through to learn about them and their goals and their finances? Just to give the reader an idea of what they would go through if they met up with you.

Chuck Price: Well, one of the segments on my radio show is I do a little spiff called Ask the Financial Doctor. I came up with that years ago and I actually went and trademarked "Ask the Financial Doctor®."

Cool.

Chuck Price: I've used that on my radio show and what we do is we run ads about getting a financial checkup with the financial doctor, me. How we do a financial checkup is exactly the way you probably go in and meet with your doctor. We have a new person that comes in, brings in all their investments, brings in their will, their trust if they have one, brings in their life insurance, brings in all their investments, and I offer a free analysis of the portfolio. But unlike a lot of my competitors, if somebody has a good program I tell them they have a good program. I don't try to replace people's stuff just because I want to get a fee or a commission. If somebody has a good program and their Advisor is doing a good job, I compliment them. To tell you a little story about this Tim, I had a guy on the radio called in and he was an elderly gentleman and he called in and he said, "I heard you say that on the radio that you do this financial checkup. Do you really do this unbiased?" I said, "Yes, I do." I said, "Because if I don't, I'm getting out of the business. If I can't be honest with you, sitting there looking you in the eye and I can't be honest with you, I need to be out of the business." He came in to see me and this guy had a portfolio over $7 million.

Wow.

Chuck Price: He had left it with me. I did an analysis. He came back the next week. I'd looked at his portfolio and I said, "Listen, in all honesty, there's nothing I can do better than you." He'd been investing himself.

I said, "In all honesty, there's nothing I could do better than you. You've done a great job of accumulating wealth and estate planning. You've done all the things I would recommend you to do." I said, "And I can't say that you didn't do them better because you probably did. You've done a great job." He looked at me and he said, "You know, you're the fourth advisor I've talked to and the other guys have radio shows too, and every one of them told me they could do better than I'm doing." He said, "The difference is I know that every one of them is a liar and you're sitting here telling me the truth." He said, "I'll tell you what,", and this guy did not look 85 years old. He said, "Listen, I'll tell you what, would it be okay with you that I give your name and card to my son and if something happens to me I want you to manage the portfolio for my son and my wife when I pass." I said, "I would be honored." I said, "But I can tell you I won't do as good as you did." He said, "That's okay, at least I know you're honest."

That tells me right there that a lot of my fellow advisors don't do that with their clients. I can tell you that probably about, I'd say about one out of 10 prospects that I meet I actually tell them, "Look, there's nothing I could do better than what you're doing. You're doing a great job. Just keep doing it. Maybe put a little more in to retire, but you've got a great strategy and what you're doing works." Because, in all honesty, there are good advisors out there and there are bad advisors out there and I believe that the majority of the Advisors want to do the right thing, although sometimes they're in a position where they can't do the right thing. But they do want to do the right thing for their client, and I think that's important. I've said that on my radio show. I've said, "Most advisors I think are good, but if you have one that's recommending you to do something and you know better, then you need to make a change."

That's a great story. I really enjoy hearing stories like that. It makes something generic like financial services and it puts it in the context of a real person and real, everyday what's going on out there.

Chuck Price: Well, I'm proud of the fact too that my son and my daughter-in-law are both in the business and I have a son-in-law in the business. My family has gravitated to the same business I'm in. Although my son is in an office right in my complex with me, but my daughter-in-law is an independent as is my son-in-law. Both of them work for firms that they work for and have done extremely well and I'm proud of all of them.

That's great.   That's really great.   You've already talked about some of the benefits of working with you and what you do, but talk more about some of the benefits that someone could get if they became one of your clients.   More than just returns and something on their statement, but more about from an emotional standpoint, a peace of mind standpoint, that sort of thing.

Chuck Price: Well, one of the advantages I think I have having been in the business for a long, long time there's virtually no market I haven't been through. Time is a tester and If you survive the test of time, that says something in itself. An advantage of our office is I probably do more educational training than anybody in Portland, and I can back that up because I'm a member of Ed Slott's Master Elite Advisor program. I have to go to two to three day training class twice a year to maintain that and there are only 270 of us Master Elite Advisors in the country that work with Ed Slott on this kind of an educated basis. I also am a lifetime member of the Harry Dent research firm, which I've been following Harry and built my practice in the 80's and 90's on his book "The Great Boom Ahead" and have been a follower. In fact, I have Harry Dent on my radio show the third Saturday every month Harry Dent calls in live and we do a half hour with either Harry Dent or his partner Rodney Johnson from Dent Research and have them actually live on the air to talk to our clients.

We keep our clients up to date. I subscribe to a lot of different information that I put out to my clients just through our weekly newsletter. We do a weekly email newsletter. We're a little different than a lot of people because we also are concerned about our client's longevity. One of the things I do is I have a nutritionist that I do a lot of work with and have her on my show on a segment we call "Investing in your Health". We've helped a lot of people turn their lives around physically, eating to give themselves longer longevity. We provide a fat burning recipe every week in our newsletter. My clients love that stuff because not only do they stay informed on the latest taxes and estate planning techniques, but we also give them something they can go make in the kitchen and eat and feel good about it because it's a fat burning recipe. We try to solve our clients' total value of self. That is wealth, health, and longevity.

That's great. That's really unusual for an advisor to branch out into nutrition and longevity, but I think it's really a part of someone's total well-being and it's fabulous that you see the bigger picture. It's not just about the dollars and the cents and the dollars on the statements.

Chuck Price: Well Tim, if you had all the money in the world and got to be age 65 and decided to retire but you had terrible health, you're not going to enjoy retirement anyhow. It's just like the guy who didn't do any investing, who reaches 65 but he's a health nut and all he ever did was eat healthy and jog but he never saved any money for retirement. What's he going to do? Eat pine nuts for retirement? I don't think most people want to do that.

No, I don't think they want to.

Chuck Price: We think it's important if you're planning on investing and saving the money for the long haul, then you also got to prepare your body for the long haul.

87

I think that's really important. I really do. I'm into nutrition myself and I definitely see the value of doing that. Let me ask you this, what's the biggest reason why you get up in the morning and go to work in your practice? You've been doing this for over 40 years. You could probably be retired yourself. What gets you still motivated to want to do what you do at Price Financial Group Wealth Management, Inc.

Chuck Price: Well, I've been to about every place I ever wanted to be and I've traveled to where I wanted to go. I've tried retirement but it's too boring for me. I cannot play golf every day and I can't sit and watch TV all day or can I see myself sitting in a rocking chair. I've got to be doing something, I've got to be using my mind. I'll tell you, the clients I have that have lived the longest are the ones who stayed engaged in something. They were doing something, they were running their own company or they volunteered at school, became a teacher or whatever, but they stayed involved. I just know to have longevity and keep your mind sharp you need to stay engaged. If you're going to be engaged you better do it in something you love to do and this business has been a great business for me to be in, been a great business for my family and it gives us something to discuss at family gatherings.

That must lead to some interesting conversations around the dinner table, the Thanksgiving table, or what not.

Chuck Price: Well, it does, but it's pretty neat because at the end of the day we all basically have the same conceptual thoughts about taking care of our client first.

I know they got that from you Chuck, after listening to what you have to say. I know that they've saw your integrity and probably continue that in their own practices. That's great.

Chuck Price: Well Tim, I've been doing this for well over 45 years and I probably shouldn't say this but when people go and check out people on BrokerCheck.org, they can see that I've never had a complaint either in the securities industry or in the insurance industry in the over 45 plus years I've been in it. I could tell you there are guys who have almost books written on them about it and I always tell the consumer, "Look, if you want to know what this guy is, you need to check him out on BrokerCheck.org. You need to also check him out with the Insurance Department and see if they have any complaints or any problems that they've had in their business because they can't hide those. Those have to be disclosed."

That's one of the reasons I joined the Better Business Bureau too because a lot of people can't get in that. I also belong to the National Ethics Association. You can't belong to that group if you've had any complaints or problems in your business. I tell people all the time, "Check the person out you're doing business with." If I'm going to give you a half a million dollars to invest for me, shouldn't I know about you and your past dealings with clients?

Definitely.

Chuck Price: Yeah. I tell clients to ask. In fact, I offer them a copy of my BrokerCheck and I offer them a copy of my information because it's crystal clear.

Well, sounds like you have a very clean record, squeaky clean as I would call it, and that's a good thing in this day and age.   As we move towards wrapping this up, is there anything else you'd like to share?

Chuck Price: No, but I would like to thank you for doing this interview with me and the professional way you went about it!

Well, good, I appreciate that. Okay, well if you don't have anything else to share we can wrap it up.

Chuck Price: Yes, but one other interesting thing is our radio show in the Portland area is we get more phone calls than the sports shows get.

Wow, that's interesting to me.

Chuck Price: I know. I know, our station manager was shocked. We talk to him about it and he said, "You guys get more calls." I said, "Because we're more interesting. We're talking about three different subjects, sometimes four. We're talking about investing, we're talking about estate planning, we're talking about taxes, and now that I have the other segment we have a nutritionist that comes on once a quarter and talks about investing in your health. Since we started doing the nutritionist in March we have had several people, a couple in Phoenix and a couple in Oregon, have lost over 24 pounds. One guy's almost lost 40 pounds since going on this nutritional plan. I can speak highly of it because I have lost over 40 pounds myself and lowered my blood sugar and my blood pressure.

That's just amazing. I hear occasionally stories like that and a lot of it is tied to nutrition. Everybody thinks you got to do 60 minutes of cardio every day and you don't. You just need to get better at watching what you eat and eating nutritional things and cutting out all the junk food.

Chuck Price: Yes it is and I have more energy.

That's one of the biggest things you can do.

Chuck Price: Well, our program that we do with the nutritionist, we eat six times a day and you're eating smaller meals but you're eating six times a day and you keep fueling your body and your body actually burns the fat within itself if you're eating the right foods. That's what we do is just eat the right kinds of foods. The cool thing is we have recipes and you can learn to do this and cook yourself. You don't have to buy special meals, you can do your cooking yourself. My wife and I cook over the weekend and cook our meals up for the whole week, and then we've got them for the whole week for me to take for Lunch and our dinners at night, we're pretty much all done.

Well that sounds like a good way to save time and not get too stressed out during the week when you're doing all the other things that you're doing.

Chuck Price: Yes it is!   It's easy when you've have food that you can grab and go because we all encounter times where we don't have time, we've got to be some-where or do something and we have things made up that we can grab and go and we're sticking right within our plan. We're not stopping and buying a cinnamon rolls at the bakery. We're eating something that's actually healthy.

Well, I really believe in what you're doing Chuck and I know you've been doing it for a long time and you talked about Investing Simplified and you've talked about investing in your health and helping people both live long in retirement as well as not run out of money. I

think that's two of the biggest things that people need help with.

Chuck Price: You know Tim, my favorite movie of all time is "Star Trek" and I have to tell you, I think that Spock the Vulcan had it right, when he says, "Live long and prosper."

That's so funny because I was thinking of that while I was saying that but I didn't really want to go there because I didn't know if it fit in, but as soon as you started going there I knew exactly what you were going to say.

Chuck Price: Yeah, but I think Spock had it right, live long and prosper. That's really what we all want to do, isn't it?

Yes, I totally agree. Okay, it's been awesome talking with you today and I appreciate all your insights. I learned a few things myself.

Chuck Price: Well listen, thanks for letting me share my insights about retirement and investing.

Okay, I really appreciate it. Thanks Chuck for sharing your insights!

Chuck Price is the founder of Price Financial Group Wealth Management Inc. which is a registered investment adviser in the states of Oregon and Washington. He is author of "Investing Simplified" – What You Don't Know Can Hurt You. He also has a radio show called "Investing Simplified". You can listen to his show at www.InvestingSimplifiedRadio.com.

The adviser may not transact business in states where it is not appropriately registered or exempt from registration. Individualized responses to persons that involve either the effecting of transactions in securities or the rendering of personalized investment advice for compensation will not be made without registration or exemption.

Chuck Price, CRFA, CSA, is Licensed for Insurance in Washington, Oregon, Alaska, Arizona & Virginia.

CONTACT INFORMATION:

Price Financial Group Wealth Management, Inc.
555 SE 99th Ave, Suite 2013
Portland, OR 97216
Phone: (503) 253-3000
Email: chuck@pfgwm.com
Website:
http://www.pfgwm.com
http://www.InvestingSimplifiedRadio.com
http://www.InvestingSimplifiedBook.com
Facebook:
https://www.facebook.com/AskTheFinancialDr
LinkedIn:
https://www.linkedin.com/groups/6937746/profile

Chapter 4
The Exponential Power of Two
by
Daryl Shankland, President, Principal Advisor, Shankland Financial Advisors, LLC
and

Buddy Nidey, Investment Advisor Representative, Shankland Financial Advisors, LLC

"Know what you own, and know why you own it."
-Peter Lynch

Okay. Hey, it's Tim Turner with Torrid Technologies and I have a couple of guests today. The first one is Daryl Shankland and she helps people determine what they can do to be sure they can retire in dignity and not run out of money in retirement. She's the president and principal of her registered investment advisory firm, which is Shankland Financial Advisors, LLC and she's been helping clients plan and manage their money since 1980. Welcome Daryl, are you there?

Daryl Shankland: Good morning. Yes I am.

Great. We also have Buddy, Buddy Nidey. Buddy's been in the tax business for 17 years and in the financial business for about four years. He uses his tax knowledge to specialize in tax strategies for retirement income planning. Buddy, are you there?

Buddy Nidey: I'm here also.

Great. Okay, let's start with Daryl. Could you tell us a little bit about yourself, Daryl? Where you grew up, any hobbies, what do you like to do, just a little bit about your background.

Daryl Shankland: Sure. As a child, our family moved around an awful lot. I was born in Worcester, Massachusetts. A tornado went through and destroyed the town when I was three months old, so we started moving. I was in six schools in grade school before settling into Elmhurst, Illinois in the Chicago area by high school. I went to the University of Illinois in Champaign-Urbana where I graduated with a degree in broadcast journalism.

I worked as a reporter for several years before moving into the sales department. I had a blast working with business owners trying to help them with their advertising, but it wasn't quite challenging enough. I discovered the investment advisory field had an awful lot of what I was looking for and considered it for a couple of years before choosing it. Then I found the ever-changing, fast-paced environment that I was really seeking and very meaningful work that I truly love.

I've been doing that since 1980. I'm one of the "old dogs" in this business and have been through a lot of cycles in the market. To relax, I love to paint. My creativity has always been a big piece of me and I've applied it in a lot of different directions. The painting really occupies my brain totally, so I forget about whatever's going on in the market when I'm working on a piece of art.

I find that if I take a little time off to do art, it does reenergize me beautifully for the business. It's all about really seeing and that's the commonality. Our clients really need us to see where they are. I think it takes a creative approach and some pretty good people skills to work with people's money. Really, it's funny. Everything you've done before filters into what you're doing now and that's very, very true in our business.

Yeah. That's interesting. My wife and I, we love to go to museums and see a lot of great paintings. What kind of painting do you do? Oils or acrylic or what?

Daryl Shankland: I do primarily Landscapes in oil and I do pastels as well. Pastels are not as forgiving outside if you have rain and we live in a rainforest up here. You've got to watch the pastels. I take them to places that are drier if I'm going to be doing on location Plein Air work. I like to do paintings that are loose and fast. It's just my personality; I don't like overly detailed paintings. I really like to pop the color in my work.

I'm a happy person by nature and my paintings do, hopefully, reflect that, but I really take in a view. I'm very satisfied working on location because there's really no way to flesh out the colors as well any other way. I also paint in my studio when I do custom work. What's wonderful about the process for me is the layers I'm putting in and how totally wrapped up in it I can get.

I am always focused on our business, of course, but it's healthy to get a break from it, a respite. I don't need another job. I work plenty of hours, so I want my painting to be totally a different part of me. Painting has really helped me get out of my head in a good way. Early on, Monet was my biggest inspiration as an artist. Later, I've been inspired painting alongside brilliant artists all over the world. Unlike Monet, I can talk with them about technique.

Monet?

Daryl Shankland: Yes, Monet. I've been to France, and have painted where both Monet and Van Gogh painted. I am a somewhat realistic impressionist. I like what Monet did with color. Of course, at the time, it was considered very controversial.

Yes. I have a picture of Giverny, where my wife and I went last summer. We love Monet. We could probably talk about this for an hour. Very interesting subject.

Daryl Shankland: I think what might be interesting to clients who get to know us is that there is an interface between art and the science of investing. I really do think it's about seeing and listening and digging deeper, because in order to have a beautiful painting, you do underpainting.

You put colors in first that are in the shadows that are underneath, that are not visible much at the end. If they're not there, you get a flat painting. Our work is like that. We really dig. It's a serious process to dig into someone's finances. It's where the rubber meets the road. When you look at the process, they're really very similar. I keep that in mind because we're working with human beings who are complex and fascinating in their lives and their finances always reflect their complexities.

Okay. Let's move on to just a story from your child-hood, Daryl, that had a big impact on your life. Tell me something that you recall that was memorable to you.

Daryl Shankland: I think the biggest lesson I learned is that it's okay to be the first one to reach out. If you're the new kid on the block, you're going to be really lonely if you sit there and wait for everybody to come to you. I was the new kid on the block a lot growing up, and I would go up and introduce myself to people and say, "Hi, my name is Daryl. I'm new here." The right people will gravitate to you if you are always genuinely yourself.

As a kid, I really learned to be true to myself. I had to be resilient. I had to be brave, and I had to overcome my own sense of shyness. Those are all great skills if you want to be in business because sometimes the other person is feeling tentative. You need to help them warm up and be all right dropping some of their masks to the outside world. That was really the central lesson as a child.

My parents were supportive, but as kids, we were all out there in schools making our way in new communities. I think it toughened us up. As a freshman in High School I started waitressing for spending money. I loved waitressing. I enjoyed the quick rapport you get with people. I learned the value of a lot of hard work and I liked having my own money.

I learned that early on. It served me well, and I liked being somewhat in control of my own money. I didn't want to be totally dependent on my parents, even as a kid. The banter with the people in the restaurants was really quick and making small talk easily was a good skill to have. That served me very well in broadcasting, which was what I ended up doing first. I initially took my creative spirit and applied it to writing. I did writing long before I did painting, but it's still all communicating.

I hear a number of themes coming through that you're mentioning about your creativity, resilience. I can tell you're a very outgoing person from the moving around and being a waitress. You have an affinity for meeting people. I hear that come through as well and also, the value of hard work, which is something that a lot of people these days don't know much about.

Daryl Shankland: They don't.

Before we move over and talk to Buddy about what his background is, tell me more about how you got in the financial business and what attracted you to that. You mentioned a little bit about it, wanting the challenge and the fast pace, but could you just elaborate on that some more?

Daryl Shankland: Sure. Back when I was still in the broadcasting business, I had moved from the news department over to the sales department and I was calling on local business owners. This was back in 1980 when brokers did not advertise. Lawyers didn't advertise back then. Nobody in the "Professions" advertised. I thought that was ridiculous because I had no idea what they did in the local Paine Webber office. So, I kept calling on the local Paine Webber manager and saying, "Hey, I think you should tell people what you do here."

He would say, "We don't advertise." I'd say, "Oh, that doesn't make sense. Surely you have an advertising budget somewhere." I would make tapes for him and write out whatever he told me it was that they did and come back to him. After about four or five visits with me, he said "I'm not going to buy advertising from you, but you are so persistent and such a pain, you would make a great broker." I remember thinking, "Gee, if being a pain is all it takes, maybe I could do that!"

Did it have to do with the name of the firm "Paine" Webber?

Daryl Shankland: Yes, somehow that made it a very good fit! He kept trying to cajole me into getting in the business because he could see in me things that I couldn't see in myself at that point. I was 28 years old. I wasn't convinced at all that I should do this business. I was very skeptical. I didn't really know anything about money. I took it upon myself to interview at every single firm in town, of course, because I'm very thorough.

I talked to all of them and they all had different flavors, and I ended up at Paine Webber because I liked the manager. He was the one who really was convincing me to make the change, and they had a great training program. My alternative at that point was to go to law school. That was what I thought I was going to originally do. Back when we were in Champaign-Urbana, I was applying to law school, but I put that on hold and had a couple of wonderful children instead.

I have no regrets there, of course, but it changed my trajectory. I was looking for meaningful work. The brokerage business absolutely offered that without having to go to law school and was totally challenging. I was very well-suited to it and I caught fire pretty quickly in that job.

I had found a career where I could have a real impact on someone's life. It was definitely a weightier kind of work than staying in the advertising field would have been or that journalism could have been in a small town. Once I was hired at Paine Webber, I went through a training program and was then out there working with folks. I used all of my media background in communication with clients.

I was the local "Suze Orman" and I was on TV a lot. I was the one that they called for an interview when the market crashed in 1987. I would sit on the set and be interviewed. All of my connections in the broadcast industry really helped me a lot in terms of getting my name out there and having people know what I was thinking and doing. I was in Quincy, Illinois, a small town. I worked there for over 30 years.

I couldn't go to a grocery store or any place and not be recognized. Television made me very visible, but it was always enjoyable. I could not have been in a career where I was bored or didn't enjoy it. I firmly believe people should find the work they're born to do and that if you do that, it's not like work. I work really long hours now. I wouldn't do that if I didn't love the work. You've got to love what you do.

Yeah. Definitely if you love what you do, you're not really working. You're doing something you enjoy.

Daryl Shankland: It's a blessing if you can find that thing that you should really be doing. Buddy and I do a tremendous amount of outreach in our communities here in the Western North Carolina mountains. We do that because we thrive on doing it. We love answering their most complicated questions, specifically on Social Security and taxes.

These are the areas that most investment people are not really addressing thoroughly with their clients. There's a big lack of information. If you can go out there and meet that need and really be thorough, it's a great way to connect with people. They have a free look at you at a seminar and listen to how you talk and interact with them. In a few meetings, we can decide together if we want to work together. When it's money, it's intimate, and it needs to be a good fit.

Yeah, that makes sense. Okay, so let's move over to Buddy. Why don't you start by sharing a little bit about yourself, Buddy, and where you grew up and just whatever you want to share?

Buddy Nidey: Sure. I grew up in the Chicagoland area and spent most of my life there. Basically, I went to school. I went to college and I managed to cram four years of college into 25 years to get my degree. I'm a little bit persistent about doing things. I worked in Chicagoland. I worked for small companies, big companies, the full gambit. I had my own business at times and always ended up in the management area in some way, shape, or form.

As you know, if you're a manager, you get involved in people's lives. I was constantly talking to people about their lives in general. They all brought their problems to me. I could never solve them, but I could at least help guide them a little bit. I've been teaching people a lot. I would always have to teach people how to do their job and how to improve their job. It was a lot of people to people contact.

I enjoy working with people and my greatest success as a manager was when one of my employees was promoted to another job. I enjoyed that quite a bit. In 2015, I came down to North Carolina and worked with Daryl. We had one project we worked on. It went really, really well, so in 2016, we moved from Illinois to the western mountains of North Carolina. We fell in love with the people here, and we fell in love with the mountains. We literally live in what we consider paradise.

Daryl Shankland: Yes. We're sitting here looking out the window right now at this beautiful view.

Now what city are you guys in?

Daryl Shankland: We are in Sapphire, North Carolina. Our office is in Cashiers.

Your office is in Cashiers?

Daryl Shankland: It's pronounced Cash'ers if you are in the south, but it's spelled Cashiers for those of us that started out as Yankees.

Yeah, I've actually been there before. Grove Park Inn is in Asheville, but there's another hotel up near you guys that's really nice. The Old Edwards Inn?

Daryl Shankland: Oh, yeah. That's in Highlands.

It's in Highlands. Yeah.

Daryl Shankland: It's all part of our stomping grounds.

Buddy Nidey: Just a few more things about me. I do enjoy sports. I'm a Cubs fan. We finally got some success there, but I'm also a longtime suffering Bears fan. They're kind of going in the wrong direction right now, but I also enjoy working with youngsters. My idea of a great week of vacation is spending a week at summer camp with about 400-500 kids...

Daryl Shankland: Bud, you're a glutton for punishment all around. You really are.

Buddy Nidey: Hey, it's great working in their lives and helping build values into them. Right now, I'm working with seven-year-old boys down here.

That's mainly football?

Buddy Nidey: No. it's a youth group that I work with called Royal Rangers.

Okay. That's awesome. Why don't you tell me a story about your own childhood? Since you like working with these kids, tell me something that impacted you from your youth.

Buddy Nidey: After I got through with my paper routes that I had for several years and my little snow shoveling job I had, my first real "job" was at McDonald's. I walked in and because I was tall for my age, they paid me a whole dollar an hour instead of 90 cents an hour. The first manager I worked with had a really big impact on me. He taught me how to provide good customer service, how to manage the business and relate to all ages of people.

He also reinforced the strong work ethic that my father showed me as I grew up. My father always was

110

working. He was working two to three different types of jobs and some he never got paid for, but he was always working. It helped me to develop my own work ethic, which I still have. I work whatever number of hours I need to do to get the job done for people. I still go out of my way to provide good customer service for our clients and dig deep into things as well.

I find it interesting how everyone's background molds and shapes them. You had this manager in this job that impacted you. From that, it reinforced a strong work ethic, but it also focused on good customer service and working with people. You say that some of the things you enjoy doing are teaching other people, managing other people, and helping them improve so that they can move ahead in their job. There seems to be a tie-in there.

Buddy Nidey: Absolutely.

Okay. Before we start talking about your current practice and all that you guys are doing, Buddy, I just want you to tell me how you particularly got into the financial business and some about your tax background.

Buddy Nidey: I worked in the corporate world as an accountant. I developed a part-time job, which I called my "fun" job. I started with H&R Block preparing taxes for people and I enjoyed it. Again, it was a lot of personal

111

interactions and I got very intimate with people talking about their finances and taxes. I kept saying to myself, "I really enjoy doing this because preparing taxes is not work."

That was fun! I was trying to figure out how I could possibly turn that into a full-time career. I just kept working it and then I'd go to work and the employees would come and talk to me about their 401k's. I'd have to explain to them how their 401K worked. I'd have to explain that a 401k is not a savings account you take money out of every time you need money. You try to put it there for long term.

Over the 17 years that I worked on taxes, eventually it worked out that I started in the financial business on a part-time basis because I would always talk to people and tell them, "Well, you need to set up an IRA. This will save you so much in taxes." They'd go off to another broker and give him the business. I was thinking, "Wait, I'd like to have that business." That's how I started on a part-time basis. Within a year, I was able to go to full-time. Then I met Daryl and now I'm even more full-time.

Now you said something that stands out to me that means you have a very special personality. It is "doing taxes is fun". That's what you just said.

Daryl Shankland: Who would say that?

There are not many people that would say that.

Daryl Shankland: He would.

I'm saying, it takes a special personality.

Buddy Nidey: Every year is a challenge and seems to always be more complex.

Yeah, they sure do. There's no doubt about that.

Daryl Shankland: Buddy's very good at solving puzzles. Taxes are just a puzzle.

Yes. Definitely. It's definitely a puzzle. Buddy, why don't you end out this little section by telling us about your background in the financial business, your CFP and licenses, and just a little bit about that.

Buddy Nidey: I received a certificate of Completion from the College For Financial Planning in Denver in 1994. I was unable to get into the business at that time, but I do feel that helps me now because of things that I learned then. I do have multiple insurance licenses in different states.

I have the Series 65 License, which means I am a fiduciary when working with our clients. That means I have to do what's best for the client, and Daryl does also. The major brokerage firms have operated under a different set of rules.

Yeah, that's a big deal. I talk to a lot of advisors. The ones that are acting as fiduciaries for their clients I feel tend to make more reasonable decisions in the client's best interest, and that's a good thing.

Daryl Shankland: Yeah, it's strange in the industry. The industry is morphing into forcing more people to act in this capacity. We don't do it because that's what we have to do, that's our mindset to begin with. Buddy and I just both feel very strongly that you should not be in this business if that's not how you feel about your clients. It just goes without saying. It's just who you should be.

We are so serious about conflicts of interest. Buddy never worked for a major wirehouse firm, but I did and I saw conflicts of interest on a daily basis there. It's frustrating. They have a hard time getting around it. They try, but they have a different culture. It's just difficult for clients to understand the difference until they have been thoroughly taken care of by a team with a different mindset. Buddy's always worked that way. He's come at people from doing their taxes as a start point. That's a very detailed, complex, and important endeavor.

Okay. Before we get into more about your practice, let's move back over to Daryl and bring us up to speed.

114

You started working with Paine Webber and now it's 2017, so a lot of stuff happened between then and now. If you could just briefly go over some of your background in the financial business and what you've been doing for the last number of years? You have a lot of experience, so can you share some of that with us?

Daryl Shankland: Yes. I started with Paine Webber in 1980. I was a registered representative or investment broker, whatever you wanted to call us back then. I was part of a small branch in a small town. That being the case, I really got to know my clients. They saw me on TV, they heard me on the radio, I did daily market commentary, and they pretty much walked in to see me from the surrounding countryside.

The trajectory of my career was pretty rapid and by 1987, I took over as the branch manager of that branch and kept my personal clients along with managing the office, which was a double job. I'm pretty tough, and I learned a lot from both sides. By 2003, that had really run its course for me. I actually left as a Senior Vice President with what was then Smith Barney.

I spent a couple of years with a fellow who I had trained in the business who'd started his own business and then started my own Registered Investment Advisory firm in 2006. I did that because I needed to be able to serve my clients the way they had wanted me to serve them all along. I found that I needed to be able to take trading discretion in order to be able to properly handle their accounts.

Some people don't know what trading discretion means. It means that I can put an order in to buy or sell on their behalf as long as it is in their risk profile without calling them first. I knew I needed to do that because over the years while I was at Smith Barney, if I wanted to get somebody out of a position, I'd have to call and say, "Look, I think it's time to sell this and buy that."

Clients would say, "Okay. Whatever you think is best." What was really served by that discussion? The client had a little bit of contact with me and I would have been explaining my thinking, but I could not act rapidly. Since I had 750 households by then, how in the world was I supposed to get everybody into a position and out of a position in a timely fashion if I had to call them first? It was just impossible.

That created a problem scenario. As an Advisor, If you are good at what you do you have a lot of clients. If you can't maneuver quickly on their behalf, it becomes a dis-advantage to the client. I realized I needed to take discre-tion, which, in general, I believe the brokerage firms do not want their brokers doing because they're worried about the legal liability. Brokers historically did not act as fiduciaries.

116

I'm not trying to speak for the brokerage firms, but I know that when I was there, they didn't let their brokers take discretion, period. I wanted to be able to properly serve people, so I set my firm up with that capability. Since we are discretionary, we can maneuver on their behalf. We do not have to call them first. Why does this matter? Let's pivot to the crash of 2008, which is still indelibly marked on everybody's foreheads at this point.

Yes definitely.

Daryl Shankland: We all remember where we were that year. By then, I had my clients all settled, and I moved them 100% to cash in January of '08 sidestepping the nasty downfall that occurred in the ensuing months. If I had not been able to exercise discretion, I could not have done that. I saved them a lot of money. They should have sent me flowers, but they didn't. They never do, but they were grateful for that move.

I had the ability to act the way I needed to act, and it had a major impact on our client portfolios. I don't pretend to always be perfect, because I'm not. If you're in the market, you've got to be able to course correct. That's the key: Be able to course correct. So, we do. We do try to communicate to clients in a timely fashion, but I don't have to call them all first and that makes a big difference in our ability to manage the money.

Going back to the differences…. Really, the standard brokerage firms are stuck with their model and therefore they do a lot of preaching of "Buy this and hold it forever." Buy and hold forever does not always work. It didn't work in 2007/ 2008. It crushed their accounts. Some people are still not at break even. I don't believe it is the way to invest. I think it can make you lazy. It can give you an excuse not to monitor portfolios.

We see antiquated portfolios all the time when we're reviewing positions that clients hold. That's not in their best interest. It can't be an excuse to make you not be on top of things. I think we really want to know that when clients come into our fold, we can take care of them in every way that's meaningful, everything from the information flow to the brass tacks of the actual portfolio management.

Those things all matter. I think that's a key takeaway. I have to do it my way now. I've been in the business so long that I know what's appropriate. If the contact doesn't have a high degree of trust with us, they're not going to become clients. It takes a while to get to know people, of course, but this is a high trust position that we're in and they should be in a high trust relationship with whoever they're working with.

We are so thorough. We get people coming in to see us who tell us after two meetings with us they've learned more than they've ever learned from their person who they've been working with for sometimes 20 years. The question is: "If their advisor is so wonderful at guiding them, why didn't that person answer all their questions about their retirement and income planning?" Why are they coming to us?

We find that they're coming to us because there's something missing in the process with their current advisor. It makes that other advisor vulnerable to losing them as a client, and they should be vulnerable to losing them. I'm all for relationships, but I'm for relationships that work, that really serve the needs of where they are now. So, why would someone be attracted to us? I think they're attracted to us because we're specifically answering their questions.

We will look at their portfolio and say, "What you have in place right now can safely generate this amount of income for you over the next 25-30 years." We dig into their budgets and we figure out what their budgets really are. Believe it or not, some people don't know their monthly need. We look for gaps and we figure out how to fill them, because you can't work until you're 110 to fill the gap.

You've got to come up with something as a solution to make sure that they're on solid footing as they say, "Okay, I'm not going to work anymore. Where's the income going to come from?" Their brokers don't seem to be able to answer that question by and large for people that come to us. That's unfortunate because they should be able to answer that question. What we realize is there's a lot of bad information out there.

Investors still think that if the market has averaged 6% to 8% for them that they can just take out 6% to 8% and that they're fine. "That's what the market's making. Why can't I just take it out at the rate that the market's making and my money holds together?" They do not know that if they take that high a distribution rate and the market declines, it will hit them harder once they retire because they have to make withdrawals. They are more or less guaranteeing that they're going to blow up their money in about eight years under certain scenarios.

Most of us, if we retire at 65, are going to live beyond eight years. A retirement income program has got to be structured to last 20 or 25 years with current longevity figures. You can't just blithely make these numerical assumptions that the average client thinks that they can make. The 4% rule used to be the withdrawal rate that advisors would recommend. That has been debunked. That is not the number anymore.

The number is closer to 2%, and that's terrifying because hardly anybody has enough money saved to be only withdrawing 2%. There are a lot of calculations we do to properly structure a portfolio. We try to give them the growth that they're going to need so they cover the inflation component, which is going to be there. We coordinate the growth with their guaranteed sources of income, which are social security, pensions, and any guaranteed incomes that they may have from the insurance company side, such as annuities and cash values within life insurance contracts.

We take that kind of planning very seriously. Bud has an amazing, magical amount of work that he throws in on his analytics to see to it that we have the numbers crunched properly. That's the piece that people are missing. They frequently have had competent advisors during the growth phase, during the asset accumulation phase where it's just all about some asset allocation and keeping you really diversified and high quality and all of that. They may have been pretty good at that.

Our area is very retirement-oriented. People move here and sometimes they're working a couple of years part-time before they're finally ready to retire. They can't get the main question answered of "Do I have enough money to retire?" They may go to their person three or four times and be totally frustrated and not get an answer, and then they come to us.

If you don't mind, can I jump in here? You've covered a lot of ground. You mentioned the 4% rule being

debunked and the importance of analyzing their situation in order to keep them from running out of money. Buddy, do you think you can talk a little bit more about how your practice is currently focused in this area? She mentioned the number crunching which I think you probably do a lot of and what the tax impacts are, the tax strategies, things that you're focusing on for the clients that you're working with.

Buddy Nidey: We look at what they tell us the figure is that they think they're going to need to live on into retirement. I'm going to take that number and figure out after taxes, "What do you need to take out to get to that number?" We create a spreadsheet for them, which we call "Income Mapping". It starts out projecting 15 years into the future. Whenever things change, we go back and redo the work on this spreadsheet.

Our goal is to make sure that they have enough income to meet their needs. We're going to show them: "We're going to take X dollars out of this bucket, and also money out of this bucket. We're going to turn Social Security on in this year." It shows how that's going to play out and is very detailed. We go month by month over that 15 year period, so it's a long five page spreadsheet. We create a personal balance sheet for them. A lot of the people that come in have never done a personal balance sheet. We see what they've got to work with.

Daryl Shankland: And their debt level.

Talk about the personal balance sheet. What's involved in that? What's in the personal balance sheet?

Buddy Nidey: We're going to sit down and get their list of what their assets are, what their liabilities are, and what the value of their house is. We come up with a reasonable value for the house. We examine their mortgage to determine when it will be paid off. Is it going to be paid off when they retire or is it going to take another five years, ten years? We adjust the spreadsheet accordingly so that we don't need as much in those later years once they've got the mortgage paid off.

Daryl Shankland: What about the inflation projections?

Buddy Nidey: Oh. I'm very conservative coming out of the accounting side. To be sure they are covered, I use a 3% inflation rate, but we do not adjust Social Security Income or anything that doesn't have a guaranteed cost of living increase. As you know, with Social Security, we only got 3/10th's of a percent increase this year. In the last couple years, it was zero. If Social Security payments do go up, they've got a bonus and we're thrilled for them.

Daryl Shankland: Right. We're happy for them. Some people have pensions with an automatic escalation

123

clause. If they worked for a really great school district, they may have a generous pension. We do encounter that on the educational side from time to time where they've got an automatic 3% hike. We do the pension analysis as well, and we can factor those in. We also make very conservative assumptions in their rate of return on their investment portfolio.

We will usually use 3% to 4% of assumed earnings there. We're not trying to actually come in at what the market tends to do over time because we want to build in some lean years in there as volatile as everything has been. We're very careful about our assumptions. Then they know what they really potentially can live on.

Buddy Nidey: We've even had some clients that have been a little more successful where we can throw in every couple years a $5,000 or $10,000 trip and still fund it.

Daryl Shankland: There are people we have to convince that they can spend more money. We have met couples who are very, very frugal. We said, "Look, you're not spending enough. You can have more fun." It's a great conversation to have. We have others that we have to say, "Oh, dear. This is not so good. You need to slow down your spending."

You're having too much fun.

Daryl Shankland: Uh, Oh. You're having too much fun! There is a phrase that we like to use which is, "Bad news does not get better with time." If that's the case, and we have to give someone bad news, we want to give it to them early enough that they can change course and amend their plans. They can work a little longer, or get more prudent in their spending, so that they're not guaranteed to fail. People don't know these numbers. They need help getting these numbers. If I didn't have Bud to do the number crunching, it would drive me crazy because I like the big picture stuff better and the investing part. He's the number cruncher.

That's great. It sounds like you guys work really well together as a team with your different skillsets. Let me start with Buddy on this one, though. I'd like you to talk about who your ideal client is and what types of people you help and then we'll let Daryl follow up with her thoughts on that.

Buddy Nidey: The ideal person is somebody who's probably going to be retiring in the next 2 months to five years, somewhere in that area. We want to examine what their Social Security benefits are going to be and if they have options to file for a benefit on a deceased or ex-spouse. Also, we look at how to take their pensions. We're going to ask them to realistically tell us what they can live on. I've had people tell me that they need $14,000 a month in retirement. I need to verify that they can do that. We also get clients who have already started their Social Security benefits but who want to examine if their portfolios should be revamped for higher security or more responsive management.

Buddy Nidey: We always want to delve into what are their personal requests. What do they see themselves doing in retirement? Some people are going to work a little bit, no matter what. But what do they want to do? What do they want to achieve? What's on their bucket list and is there a way to get them to fulfill that bucket list? Again, we keep it very personal. Every client is different, and everyone's got different wishes. We've had some people who want to set up a legacy. We've had other people that tell us, "I want the last check to the nursing home to bounce."

Daryl Shankland: Yeah, it's really interesting. Where we are working, we have everything from Beverly Hillbillies to Beverly Hills. It's just the nature of the environment. We do really try to meet people where they are. We have no client minimums and we do a lot of outreach into the community specifically on Social Security planning seminars, which is a big need. People are just not aware of what the resources are, and the Social Security offices can't do planning.

They can tell you what you're qualified for right now. They can do the paperwork, but they won't do advice and strategy. Advice and strategy is exactly what we do. We do incorporate all the guaranteed pieces that we need into this. Really, the ideal client is someone who is receptive going through the process. People appreciate the amount of time we put into the process and we do it without charging them our normal hourly fees.

There are times when an hourly fee might be on the table, but it's generally not on the table for our normal planning. If the clients can bring us a good list of their assets and can provide statements, we can usually delve right into the income mapping report. Sometimes they don't have good records and everything's a mystery. Sometimes one spouse has been totally in control of the assets and is now incapacitated or gone. Then, we might have to spend some time reconstructing what they have first.

In general, those are free consultations. By the end of a two hour first meeting we have a very good handle on where they are, and they know us better by having gone going through the process. At that point, they're receptive to moving forward with us or they're not. We part friends if it is not a good fit, but obviously, we're in the business to do work for people. We like giving of ourselves first and asking for a commitment from them after they've gone through the process with us.

127

We think it's a good way to work. We've both been mature enough in our businesses for long enough that we can afford to do that. That's a really nice thing because it takes the pressure off of those meetings. They're not feeling like the clock is ticking and it's going to be $2,000 before they get an answer, which a lot of people are not going to spend. Even if they have money, they don't want to spend it because people with means are notorious for being frugal. That's why they have it!

Nobody wants to spend the money, even though they all need the advice. We like the work to be structured in a non-pressured way.

People realize with us that they have the yin and yang of the Daryl and Buddy team, because we're very different personalities. Buddy sometimes has a hard time getting a word in edgewise because I come from broadcasting and I love to talk. When he does say something, it generally is important. The work that he does is critical on taxes and income analytics, and it is very intertwined with the investment pieces.

I'm analytical regarding the investment management side. I want to communicate both the specifics and the broader concepts of their investment portfolios. I'm also making the primary day to day decisions on the maneuvering of the portfolio. As a team, we have to split up the work or we'd both be just drowning.

128

Buddy does hypothetical tax returns to illustrate the impact of a potential decision. When we're in a discussion and we're trying to look at the tax impact, he will quickly dig in and do a dummy tax return right then and there. We know the answer to the question of what the tax cost is right away because he's really adept at that. Because both of us have our specialized areas, the meetings become really meaty informational meetings for most people.

Whatever comes up, odds are that Buddy's going to sit there and Google some kind of research, handing them valuable information about something that comes up in the discussion.

We are living in the perfect place. Our ideal clients are all around us here because they're all retirees, pre-retirees, and people who've lived other places and are adventurous enough to have moved here just like we did.

We're meeting people on a daily basis who we would have as friends. It's just a delightful way to work. The relationship has to be a good fit from both sides. Honestly, if somebody doesn't like us and they don't like the chemistry of what we do, odds are we don't like them either. It's just best to admit that.

We tell them in our seminars, "If you don't like who we are up here, it's okay not to make an appointment because this is who we are. What you see is what you get. If that's not appealing to you because of personalities or whatever, it's okay. Find someone that you can do this with because chemistry is pretty critical to the process."

Okay, so you've talked a lot about what you do to help your clients. We've got working with them on their social security, we've got a personal balance sheet, we've got tax implications and strategies. Could you just give us a structure of when you start to work with someone, how many meetings do you have? What do you do before they become a client versus after they say, "Yes, I want to get serious with this"? I'm not looking for a five page treatise, but just an overall structure of how you work with the clients.

Daryl Shankland: Initially, during our first couple of meetings, we will have a handle on where their money is, what they're worried about, what their income need is, and the basics of their scenario. If they decide to come on board with us, the next step is we need to transfer their assets in from wherever they are so that they go to the custodian that we use. We hold their assets at TD Ameritrade, a very big, internationally known custodian.

We transfer the money in and we make TD Ameritrade our first stop. At that point, I take over the management of the accounts and make any changes that need to be made in terms of buying and selling and getting the portfolio current with our thinking. At that point, we also do illustrations. Buddy is very involved in this part, determining which dollars might need to go over to the guaranteed income side.

In that case, we are working with insurance companies to provide lifetime income benefits or at least to anchor that money in products where there is no downside risk. We use a lot of fixed index annuities for that piece. Which ones we use do vary a lot from client to client, because they all need different bells and whistles. We do a lot of analysis at that point to determine how much money ought to be in guaranteed products and how much should be over on the investment side. The investment side covers certain areas that need covering, such as liquidity and inflation hedges that people also need.

Depending upon the client and their income need, they can be tilted more toward guaranteed income. If they really don't have that much saved and they're going to stress out their portfolio with their withdrawals, they may need to be more on the guaranteed side. We may have to adjust how much can be on the invested side. Buddy is very risk averse. He'd be the first one to tell you that we have to be realistic in our assumptions.

I love stocks. I've always loved stocks. I love what they can do to build wealth over time. Therefore, I'm the appropriate person to be running the portfolio. Buddy, of course, is critical on the spreadsheets, the number crunching and the illustrations. Ultimately, both of us are providing the data into the next series of meetings. which map out what the clients can derive from their accounts.

We basically put the pieces into place and start to turn on the money from each bucket whenever it is appropriate. It does usually involve us taking over the management of their assets. From time to time, we run into a person or a couple where somebody is really good at their own management of their assets. That's not that unusual up here. We've got a lot of bright people who've been doing it on their own for many, many years. They don't want to turn over the management to us.

That's okay. Then, we just structure the complementary pieces that need to be put into place. We still do their spreadsheet work for them, and we recommend the guaranteed income pieces. What those guaranteed income allocations generally do is replace what we used to position into bonds. These discussions can have real "light bulb" moments.

If investors realize where they're currently sitting in terms of the overall economic scenario we are now in, with historically very low rates, they know that at some point rates are going to start to tick up. If they're sophisticated enough to know how bonds work, they know they are in jeopardy of their bonds falling in value in the market. That's the piece that we really don't want them to be suffering with. It's the bond piece that we have to look at to restructure, generally.

That can be where the fixed index annuities come in. They do a very good job of replacing the safety that bonds used to provide to a portfolio and no longer can provide, in my opinion. We will frequently find a client with a lot of bonds because they've been in a "growth and income portfolio." They've got 50% of their portfolio ready to get really hurt and they don't know it.

It's certainly not what they signed up for on the bond side, to have a lot of volatility. They may be about ready to walk into some very bad years there. The overall, big picture is critical, and so we've had many clients who hire us to do the guaranteed income piece to get their bond piece cleaned up and they still manage their assets. If that's what works for them, that's okay. If the spouse in charge dies after we have worked with a couple, we've developed a relationship with the remaining spouse. They know who they can go to for help in managing the money.

Obviously, it can be the husband or the wife who's the brainiac managing the portfolio. Whoever that was can be transitioned over to the new team when that person's no longer in place to manage it. They are generally grooming us to be in place for whenever that time comes.

We can play an important role in the continuity of their financial plans.

Or perhaps it's just that they have a health issue that prevents them from continuing to be as attentive to their portfolio as they have all those years. They realize it's time to transition over to someone else.

Daryl Shankland: Yes. That happens a lot, or the spouse realizes that their spouse who's been running the money is not able to do it. They realize it before the person is willing to admit it, and they engage our services to get it under control. That's a tricky wicket, as you can imagine, but when you're dealing with people going into their retirement years, we do run into that.

The person at some point is usually willing to admit, "This is becoming too much. We're having a rough time. We really need some help." We are flexible enough to cover the pieces that we need to cover. Buddy will do the Income Tax Preparation for incoming clients.

I'd like to ask Buddy a high-level question about, and Daryl, you may want to contribute as well, but since Buddy's involved in this piece, just at high level, how do you decide how much someone needs to put on the guaranteed income side into annuities, for example?

134

Buddy Nidey: There are a whole group of things that come into that. One is how much they have available, what their dollar need is, and how much risk they can handle. Many of them that come in now say, "I never want to lose another dime in the market." They've gone through it. They've lost it. As a general rule, we might want to put maybe 50% in a fixed income product and 50% in the market and manage it properly. That can vary, again, depending on client. We don't want to put all their money into a fixed income product that locks it up for a long period of time. They need access to at least some of the money, and that's where the investment piece comes in.

Daryl Shankland: That's correct. It's really a liquidity issue. We've had clients come in and they love what we're doing with them on the annuity side so much they say, "Let's do all of that." We say, "You cannot do all of that, even though we know you are risk-averse." We can manage the portfolio from a risk-averse standpoint, but they have to have access to money in case of an emergency. With the lifetime income planning work that we do on the guaranteed side, they can access generally 10 per cent per year for emergencies.

You are essentially making a contractual arrangement with an insurance company to have your back, and there are rules of the road on that. We've got to make sure that we have access to the proper amount of money for emergency issues. That's also heavily regulated and audited. We would not pass compliance reviews with insurance companies if we were overly aggressive in how much we want to allocate to the index annuity side, so we're very aware of that.

We want to be doing this properly, so sometimes all we have to do is wrestle control of their investment piece so that it's not as volatile. Maybe their person just wasn't very talented at tamping down the volatility on the investment piece. There are techniques we can use to do that. It's not a perfect world, and we have to course correct when necessary, but when the person doesn't want much risk, we structure the portfolio accordingly.

It's not by using bonds. We're using other techniques and proper diversification. Asset allocation is critical, but there are mutual fund managers out there and entities out there that are doing very esoteric work that we plug into for clients. They are doing very interesting strategies that help keep volatility down. We like to have our clients participating in that. We're always watching out for who's really good at that because we can go anywhere with the money.

I can manage it personally and buy all their individual stocks if that's what they want. Frequently, we are plugging into other teams, mutual funds, exchange traded funds and the like to make sure they are really diversified. Maybe they're still in a very moderate to low risk with their investment assets. Once we get people properly positioned for income, sometimes they can afford to take more risk on the investment side to improve the performance. It varies with each family.

We have people come to us who have money at Fidelity and Vanguard and in their 401k who have been doing very well. They've had a set list of mutual funds that they're allowed to buy in there and that's all they've done, and they've done very well. We can bring a lot of those funds in, keep some of them, shift as many as we need. Some people are very comfortable with the amount of risk they're running on their investment side, particularly once they know we've truly diversified them with the proper allocation of the income side of their money.

Depending upon your age, the payout off of the guaranteed income side is generally going to be higher than what we can comfortably take off of their investment side. That's the magic of it. If you get that balance right overall, sometimes we can get people above a 4% distribution rate, which they may need in order to hit their income goals.

We can't usually distribute 4% in good conscience from just an investment portfolio. There's a concept called "Sequence of events risk" that enters in that's a very scary thing. If all your retirement funds were invested in the market and you retired right before the crash of '08, you were in trouble. You just lost 40% of your investment portfolio and you were taking income out on a consistent basis. You just blew up your chance for the money to last the rest of your life.

We do analysis. We show people what sequence of events risk can do to them if they have a couple of weak years early on in their retirement, and then we show them what it looks like having some of their money over on a guaranteed side generating income without any downside risk. When you blend those two, that's where you get the sweet spot. That's where you get the math that has a greater possibility to work for the average person or the above average person.

If they're really poor and all they have is Social Security and no savings, they've got a rough road ahead of them. There's nothing that we can really do to help them strategize. We're very kind about it. We do everything we can to get them the resources, government-subsidized housing, etc. We show people all of that, but they're not really clients.

Something happened to them along the way where they weren't able to save anything, so there's nothing to protect. They're just in trouble and that's very sad. We do see that. Most Americans don't have enough saved for retirement and culturally, it's a problem. We can't help them. It's too late.

It sounds like one of your magic abilities is being able to balance the part of someone's portfolio that's in investments versus annuities and related guaranteed income contracts. To be able to figure out what that balance is for each individual client is a very detailed exercise in determining how to do that.

Daryl Shankland: It is. It's the work that they need, and they don't know that they need that work done until they sit down with us. Then they say, "Oh. This is exactly what we needed to see." People just aren't aware of it. They're not on the inside of our business. This business is filled with jargon and confusion. We're trying to clarify. Somebody's got to crunch the numbers for them. They don't know what their number is, do they, Bud?

Buddy Nidey: They might have some idea, but they're not really sure. We sit down and really delve into things. Sometimes they're not even sure how much they're going to need to live on and we have to delve into that.

Daryl Shankland: Right. We had a couple who came in who were used to making $150,000 a year in their two jobs. The husband told us they only needed $1500 a month to live on! We said, "Oh, okay. Let's see. Have you been saving $7,000 a month?" People don't know how much they spend a month. They just don't. We're here to tell the truth about what we see, with kindness of course.

We're also here to give them the answers on, "Okay, how do we get you from your current place to where you really need to go?" For most people, we can do that. Generally, most of the folks that go through the process end up with a solution at the end. We're happy to be able to see that. They know that if they've got an issue, we'll strategize with them. "Okay, I'm going to have to take a part-time job. I can't stand doing what I do any longer." We get that.

There was a point where I had to leave Smith Barney and start my own company. It had run its course for me. I loved what I did there, but I wanted a different flavor. It didn't mean I got out of what I was doing, I just changed it so I liked it again. You can do that. I really encourage people to do that. We're coaches for that. I'm thinking of another person who worked at a grocery store and she really wanted to work with the elderly.

We said, "You can do that. You can go from working at the local grocery store to doing work with the senior population." We frequently get into conversations that honestly, on the surface, don't have anything to do with their money, but have everything to do with their lives. That's where sensitivity and the counseling comes in.

140

Those are all skills that draw on where Buddy and I have both been over the years.

Buddy's worked with children. He's been in a teaching capacity, and so have I at the college level. I have had children, but I haven't worked with children. Actually, I couldn't be a teacher. They would drive me nuts in a school setting. I love my children. I don't want to work with 30 of them at once. I'm not patient enough for that. God bless the teachers out there. I don't know how they do it, but I really think the process that we're going through with clients is teaching them about their scenario.

We're talking to people who know a lot about what they want and what they want to do. They're just not sure how they get from point A to point B. The process takes a little time. It's not onerous. It's generally two or three meetings where both of us are present. We gather the data and we do meaty discussions, and then we start to gather the assets and revamp the money.

In the course of a month to two months, they're off and running. They really know where they are. At that point, it's an audible sigh of relief that we get from them. It's the kind of moment when they say, "Oh, my. We really are okay." One of the members of the couple might have been saying "We're fine. I know we're fine." The other spouse was saying, "But I don't get it. I don't see it.

I don't understand." Until they see it in black and white, they do not really understand, and they do not feel secure. It takes a lot of pressure off their relationship to have good understanding. It's also making them talk to each other about what their budget really is.

We can only imagine what some of those discussions might be like that we don't see, but it's making them say, "Okay, where are we REALLY on the spending?" Has somebody got a spending problem? Those subjects can come up and we can sense the tension there. That's not our role. They're going to have to work on that on their own. Once they see the reality of the scenario, usually it will get the person who is in denial about the spending to realize where they need to reign it in.

You mentioned the clients, some of them don't know what they don't know, so to speak. When you come in, you're opening their eyes as to new ways of doing things. Talk about some of the popular misconceptions related to annuities and fixed index annuities and that area. I think that touches on an area that a lot of people have been misinformed both on the radio and on the internet as to how they work and what some of the drawbacks are versus how good they can be for providing income for people in retirement.

Daryl Shankland: I think you always want to start this looking seriously at what is someone's potential conflict of interest. There's Ken Fisher who loves to get on TV or the Internet and say he hates annuities, right? I think that's a comment that is narrow minded and over simplified at best.

However, if you know that Fisher's firm is just a registered investment advisor, you know their goal is to manage money. Their inherent conflict of interest is that they want to manage all of the money. That's what they do. They don't do annuities. You know where their bias is. For good or for bad, it's not their business model.

We really don't like to bash any one particular part of the financial industry. Everything out there has its own flavor and its own purpose in a portfolio. The pieces serve different objectives that the other pieces cannot efficiently fill. I think the big misconception is that you could buy an annuity, turn it on to income, get one check and die, and all of the money stays at the insurance company. I think that's the biggest misconception. That's not how we structure annuities in today's world. My grandmother, by the way, had one like that. She had a lifetime annuity. She made out like a bandit.

Annuities are not the same products from years and years ago. They're much more sophisticated now. These are used as tools to do heavy lifting in a portfolio on the income side. They're no more like the old annuities of the past than our cell phones are now like the phones that we used with rotary dials 30 years ago.

Annuities have advanced and are now more consumer-friendly and more flexible. The product design has improved dramatically even over the last five years, which is to the advantage of the consumer. I think the goal is to have some education for people to truly get a handle on what an annuity can do for them. In our meetings, we go from people having their arms crossed and saying, "I don't know. I don't really like the sound of annuities," to "Wow. I see what they do. I see why you're looking at them for me."

We have had people say, "Well, why wouldn't we put all our money there?" Because no one product can do everything for everybody. We have to let each thing do what its specialty is. It goes back to what Peter Lynch said, "Know what you own, and know why you own it. " It is true of individual stocks, and it is true of annuities. Where the annuities are strong is in downside protection and in generating predictable, lifetime income. That can be structured any number of ways. It doesn't necessarily have to be a guaranteed lifetime income payout. It might be just taking a systematic withdrawal or occasional withdrawals from a protected base that cannot decline.

Variable annuities are a different animal entirely. In general, we would say we don't like most variable annuities because they don't have enough downside protection. Without getting deep into the weeds about stuff that will make everybody's eyes glaze over, just know we might not like an annuity with really huge internal costs that doesn't have the proper downside protections. We are picky about what we recommend.

There are many that we do like. They are the product that fits what the client needs, that fits the goal. Some are better suited to legacy planning, some are better suited to a death benefit for an heir than others. Others are better suited to the maximum income payout. Buddy, you might want to address something here. Once we've shown a solution to someone, why wouldn't they take our advice?

Buddy Nidey: There are some cases where we run into people that are just paralyzed by fear. They lost over half their money in prior years. They had supposedly the best advice that they could get and it hasn't worked out well. They're just afraid of doing anything right now.

So mainly fear of losing money in the market.

Daryl Shankland: Or fear of just facing their true choices. It can be a lot to take in. When you know how the annuity protects you, you would think that that would be what they've been looking for. Sometimes they're just not able to digest the information and they're just afraid of doing anything. In general, when we get that, we realize we haven't built their trust yet. They just may not know enough.

We sometimes see somebody in a seminar and we do their Social Security maximization report. They don't re-tire for a year and a half and we don't see them for a while. We are talking to them over that year and a half, but they're not always ready to do business with us right away. That's all right. We are patient. We are very willing to take our time with folks, but if we get to somebody who really is at a point where they just can't make a deci-sion, then we find we can't help them.

Monitoring your portfolio involves frequent deci-sions. I'd hate to have anybody think that their money is ever something that could be in a "Fix it and forget it" kind of program. There's really no such thing. What we do see is an impact from 2008. We see a lifetime kind of event that is the equivalent of what people went through in the Great Depression in terms of the indelible mark that they have inside of them having lived through that and the consequences of that: bankruptcy, businesses lost, homes lost, etc. Investing intelligently for the long term does not mean never making a decision to get out of a position.

It's understandable that we've had a lot of fear fac-toring into today's investment world. We are in a news-oriented, 24 hour cycle now. Everything is revved up to keep everybody tuned in and it's counterproductive to planning, honestly, but it's the world we live in. At some point, we've got to be calm and very real about it, be reassuring about what the numbers look like and move forward to get a plan in place.

Burying your head in the sand on this is really not a good plan. This you can imagine. People do get frozen in that stance sometimes, or they just say, "Well, over the long haul, it will work out." But what do you own for the long haul? Will it work out? I don't mind raising that question because we have to be a devil's advocate in that kind of thinking. We absolutely have to say, "Are you sure you're comfortable? Have you really looked at it?" and get them a little bit off dead center.

One thing's for sure. The media fuels a lot of fear and gets people too focused on the swings of the market. They're on a news cycle and they've got to talk about something today, something that they can get people's attention with.

Daryl Shankland: There's a lot of garbage out there. Our emails are full of "The market's going to crash on August 23rd. Get out now." Just crazy stuff. We sometimes get calls until we get clients trained to know "Ignore all that. Please delete that. Delete, delete." We're always looking at what will drive the market. I love news. I love politics, I love all of this. I'm a big digester of all of that. But I don't overreact to hype.

I'm looking for what can move a market. What would change the tide out there? What would really have an impact on our clients' portfolios? I am watching that. I absolutely am. In 2016 there was a conventional wisdom that if Trump were elected, the market would crash immediately. That conventional wisdom was incorrect. You can't necessarily guess how it's going to react. It's a humbling force to deal with the market.

We're not here to guess what the future is going to be. We are here to pay attention and course correct when we need to, and have proper investment strategies in place that are grounded in good research. It's always good to diversify. People know not to put all their eggs in one basket, but sometimes they tell us they have 100% of their 401K in their company stock. We're horrified to see that.

Not only are their jobs dependent upon their company, but so is their net worth. How would you have liked to have worked for Enron? You lost your job and all your money if it was all in Enron. There are lessons to be learned from history. We see this. We see this with Procter & Gamble employees, Chevron employees, etc. I don't care who you work for.

With big companies, sometimes people have a disproportionate amount of their money in their company stock and they shouldn't, in our opinion. Now, they can listen to us on that or not. Sometimes they're very comfortable with it because they work there and they know the company is fine, but it's not proper diversity. If they're going to insist on holding all of their company stock for their life and do nothing to diversify, probably they're not going to be a client because we can't help them.

It's all okay. We're still going to continue the process of telling people the truth as we see it. Those truths are based on years of training, years of experience, years of going through this with clients and a lot of market cycles. I'm not someone to just say, "Oh, it'll be fine. Don't do anything. Don't worry, it'll be fine."

I'm much more likely to say, "Actually, at any given moment, every portfolio needs work." Every portfolio probably needs the losers culled out of there so that the winners can continue to run. If you will do that, you will have a stronger and stronger portfolio instead of always selling your winners and holding your losers hoping that they'll recover whereby you end up with pile of not so great stuff.

It's proper investment management that people need, and hopefully that's where we can be of help to them. Most people are receptive to it. We do transition a large percentage of the people that we meet with into becoming clients. They are relieved to have our input. It's very rewarding to be able to help them move into another phase of their lives.

That's great. I can really sense the excitement you guys have for what you do. Let's move towards wrapping this up with you telling me and everyone what the biggest reason is why you get up in the morning and go work in your practice instead of painting or just spending time in the wonderful incredible outdoors in Western North Carolina. What gets you fired up and continues to have you going to the office every day, if you could both share that?

Daryl Shankland: I can't wait to dig in and meet new people and get to the bottom of what it is that they need. We're really puzzle solvers here and it's an exciting challenge. It's not like work. We get to know people. We get up in the morning and we talk to friends all day. It's a great job.

We're thrilled to be able to give people the peace of mind of them having really had a thorough look at their situation. The people that we deal with here in the mountains are just a wonderful bunch. It's all about solving problems. I do paint, but I work more than I paint because it's still fun for me.

150

For me personally, being able to do this with Buddy by my side is the best ever. Our approaches to it, based on our personalities, are different and we know that we really flesh it out. He has my back and I have his, so it makes it not as lonely as I was when I ran the practice totally by myself for several years. It's really a joy. We have other members of the team who are a pleasure to work with as well, and they all specialize in the pieces that are closest to their hearts.

Buddy Nidey: With me, it's just a matter of every day I get up and say, "Who can I help today? Who can I make an impact in their life today?" I want to serve people. I've got a servant's heart. Helping them and seeing them succeed is what our real reward is. Seeing them be able to move into retirement, still enjoy their life, still able to take the trips that they want to take. Seeing them succeed is our greatest benefit.

Daryl Shankland: We work around the western North Carolina Mountains here, and we live in Sapphire. Our office is in Cashiers at the Crossroads. We leave the mountaintop and we drive down to Brevard, Hendersonville, and Asheville to cover those areas as well. We go out. When Buddy and I are on our way to go see people, we're driving through this gorgeous scenery.

It's not rush hour traffic. When the mountain laurels are in bloom, I'll come around a corner, just about running off the road because I see something that my artist's eye wants to stop and paint. We're on our way to a meeting, and I'm thinking, "Oh, the light is beautiful. I wish I could stop." It's just eye candy. We have this relaxing drive through the mountain and it's really nice everywhere up here.

The only time that's not so much fun is when it really is foggy. We've had that happen a couple of times. We've coming back at night in fog, and that's not so good for driving. That's about the only downside to getting out there, some of the nasty weather that you can get in any environment. We live in a place that's beautiful year-round. Our winters are not too fierce. We're venturing out year-round. I realize I'd be really bored if I weren't doing this.

In fact, I had the choice of just scaling the business down or revving it up. I chose to rev it up because I was bored. I did not have enough stimulation during the day just sitting at my computer watching the markets. It's probably a little sad to admit that I bore that easily, but I guess I do. We want to have an impact here. We want to be good members of our community and be fully engaged in this area.

We're both very active at our churches. I was co-chair of the church bazaar one year and then I realized after that, "Gee, is this how I should be spending my time? Really? With my accumulated knowledge, what's the greater gift to the community?" I can tell you it's not running the church bazaar. I love the things that I do for the church, but they have other people who can do that.

There just aren't that many people who are doing the work that Buddy and I do together like we do it. That's our gift back to the community. Many people we do analysis for have no potential to be clients. That's okay. We're happy to do it. Some of the best meetings are the meetings where they leave and we've provided clarity to a difficult situation.

It's not always about making money in this business. We believe that the money naturally follows if you take good care of people.

I have to underline that because I would encourage anyone going into retirement to really think about when they do leave their job, what's their day going to be like? Their spouse is going to be in shock if all of a sudden they're there all day and their spouse is not used to having them around. What are they now going to do with their talents and their treasures? How are they going to spend their time?

For us, that's been a really interesting journey. We found we needed to use our work skills to make our day in and day out life as meaningful as it is. We would want anyone else to do that, too. There's something they want to do. We just want to see to it that we can get them set up to be able to do that special thing. That's the joy of it for us.

That's great. I think that really comes through, the idea of serving other people, helping other people and mainly with their retirement and their finances, but not just that. You guys seem to go way beyond that and help people explore the other issues and things that they need to think about as they transition into retirement. I just want to say thanks for spending time with me today and sharing all your thoughts about your practice. I just wish you guys much success in the future.

Daryl Shankland: Thanks so much. It's been really fun talking to you.

Buddy Nidey: Thanks for having us. We appreciate it.

Okay, great. Thanks again for contributing your expertise to this book!

Daryl Shankland has been guiding clients in their investment decisions since 1980, encompassing both good times and bad. Her broadcasting background has helped her communicate complex, quickly changing information to clients in a manner that they can understand. Daryl has been a frequent commentator on financial matters on both television and radio. She served as branch manager of the Quincy, Illinois Smith Barney branch for many years before leaving to start her own firm. With her deep experience in management and client portfolio structuring, she understands how emotions can take their toll and how critical it is to trust your financial advisor.

As an Accountant and a graduate of the College of Financial Planning in Denver, Colorado, Buddy Nidey applies his strong analytical to his work as an investment advisor representative. He enjoys coordinating clients' investment portfolios with solid financial planning that takes income taxes, diversification and safety into consideration. Bud also assists clients with income tax preparation, health, life and long term care insurance as part of his financial consulting services.

Together, Daryl and Buddy work to educate their nearby communities with outreach on various topics of financial literacy. They conduct frequent workshops on Social Security Maximization, Taxes in Retirement, and Retirement Income Planning in public venues and for area businesses. They are both members of the Society for Financial Awareness, a not for profit organization dedicated to financial education.

This book is limited to the dissemination of general information regarding its investment advisory services to residents of the United States and residing in states where providing such information is not prohibited by Applicable law. This book shall not be construed by any consumer and/or prospective client as SFA' S solicitation to effect, or attempt to effect, transactions in securities, or the rendering of personalized investment advice for compensation.

Furthermore, the information resulting from the use of this information should not be construed, in any manner whatsoever, as the receipt of, or a substitute for, personalized individual advice from SFA. Any subsequent, direct communication by SFA with a prospective client shall be conducted by a representative that is either registered or qualifies for an exemption or exclusion from registration in the state where the prospective client resides. For information pertaining to the registration status of SFA, please contact the United States Securities and Exchange Commission on their website at www.adviserinfo.sec.gov.

A copy of SFA's current written disclosure statement discussing SFA's business operations, services, and fees is available from SFA upon written request. SFA does not make any representations as to the accuracy, timeliness, suitability, completeness, or relevance of any information prepared by an unaffiliated third-party.

Daryl B. Shankland   Buddy L. Nidey

CONTACT INFORMATION:

Daryl B. Shankland, Principal Advisor
Cell: 217-494-0439
Fax: 828-743-7546
Email: darylshank1@gmail.com
Buddy L. Nidey, (IAR)
Cell: 815-210-5503
Fax: 855-884-1851
Email: budnidey@sbcglobal.net

Please visit our website
at www.shanklandfinancial.com for further information
on additional team members and how to contact

157

Chapter 5

Increase Your Retirement Fund at No Cost

by

Joe Pereira

"Do unto others as you would want them to do unto you." - Luke 6:31

"Love thy neighbor as thyself." - Matthew 22:35

- The Bible

Okay. Hey, it's Tim Turner. I'd like to introduce you to Joe Pereira. He's been in the financial business for about 30 years, and his firm is called Legacy Planning. He specializes in working with families to plan their future and avoid tax and inflation pitfalls. Welcome Joe.

Joe Pereira: Yes.

Great, glad to have you on this call today, and just wanted to get started by having you share a little bit about yourself, where you're from, where you grew up. That sort of thing.

Joe Pereira: I was born in Palmerton, Pennsylvania, but I really grew up in Miami, Florida. In my early years, I served as a medic in the 82nd airborne, and then I went to Rutger's University School of Business. After I graduated from there, I headed to Miami. I've been in Miami now, and working with kids and coaching activities in the youth activities at my church for over 25 years. And again, mainly working with families and elderly people to keep as much of their finances as they can away from the IRS.

Well, that's great. That's interesting. Can you tell me, you mentioned there that you coached youth sports. What kinds of things are you coaching? I'm just curious.

Joe Pereira: I coached middle school, which is 6th, 7th, and 8th grade, football and flag football and basketball as a volunteer at our church school. I coached girls fast pitch softball in the Khoury League, sort of like Little League. Nowadays I'm the manager of our team and commissioner of the men's softball league.

I ask because I've coached youth sports for like 13 years so that's the main reason I was asking. I have a real passion for that my self -

Joe Pereira: Yeah, I like working with kids.

Good, yeah, I do too. Well let's talk about being a kid. Do you have any story maybe from your childhood that had a big impact on your life that you can think of?

Joe Pereira: Yes. My parents were both immigrants. My dad from Portugal. My mother from Czechoslovakia. I think it's not a one-time impact. I think it was watching them work and feed five kids and never stray from the path of doing right. That's it.

Okay, well tell us how you got into the financial business. What kind of attracted you to it?

Joe Pereira: I was initially a zone manager for a bunch of franchise restaurants and as I did that I ran across a guy who was in the financial business. He wanted to talk to me about it and .Introduce me to it. When I found out I could do it independently, use my education and still do my other things without any other interference, I made the move.

What are you currently focused on in your practice?

Joe Pereira: Right now I concentrate on retirement planning As part of that I have a unique program where people can pay off their mortgage years earlier and create a tax-free retirement account all using the same exact money they're paying on their current mortgage.

That's pretty interesting. Can you tell me a little bit more about how you do that? I mean, we don't have to get into super technical details but just at a high level.

Joe Pereira: It's basically a refinance of your home through a 30-year line of credit combined with a zero balance checking account. Your income is deposited into the checking account. All funds deposited in the checking account are applied to your principal balance. This immediately lowers the interest calculation. After paying your monthly bills the difference remains as a credit against your principal over the years the interest saved enables to have the mortgage paid. By continuing to make your mortgage payment direct to your reserve account creates a tax free additional retirement fund.

Well, that sounds pretty interesting. Can you tell me who your ideal client is for this type of service?

Joe Pereira: This type of service is basically for people between 40 and 60 years old. The youngsters start to pay off the mortgage earlier while not having to make any extra payments. At the same time they are starting their reserve fund. Which can be used for kids going to college For the people over 50, it gets their mortgage paid off before they retire as well as adding to their retirement funds..

But typically the youngest you work with is more in the 40-ish range?

Joe Pereira: This works best for a young family but helps every age. The major limitation is time as that affects the time the reserve fund grows

Okay. What other problems can you help people solve besides just working with their mortgages.

Joe Pereira: Analyzing where they have 401K's and IRA's to see if it is advantageous to convert them to Roth IRA's and life insurance plan. This creates a tax free fund so that when they do retire and start collecting Social Security they pay less income tax. The less taxable income they have in retirement will reduce and even eliminate the amount taxed.

What about college planning? How can you help in that area?

Joe Pereira: For college planning we have a program which tells you exactly how much it costs to send a kid through college, what potential scholarships and things are available and how they can move their assets to increase the amount of money then can get from the schools.

Okay. You've also mentioned helping people with their budgeting. What are you doing in that area?

Joe Pereira: I don't really do any Money Management.. I get with them and teach them how to do budgets and how to handle their money.

Right, I gotcha. Right, it's not investment management.

Joe Pereira: I'm not securities licensed and don't do traditional "money management" or investment management.

Yeah, correct. Okay. Okay. Let's talk about, and you've already kind of touched on this in a couple different ways but we're going to keep hammering it home just so everyone that listens to this or reads your chapter, understands how do you help your ideal client solve their problem and what is your magic expert ability that you can do for them?

Joe Pereira: Mainly, if they're willing, and it has to be how willing they are to maybe start to think outside the box, I can suggest unique concepts that apply to them. It's just I love doing it. I feel personally responsible when I'm working with them and I know I have to live with them a long time. So, what's best for them, that's the way we have to go.

People have all kinds of different problems. There's no one unique solution. No one standard solution. They really need unique, personal solutions.

So, typically you meet with a client and you analyze their finances and their goals and then you come up with come up with ideas in areas where you might be able to help them with.

Joe Pereira: Right. Specific to their situation. Everybody has a different problem but in the end it boils down to what's going to happen when I retire if I keep doing what I'm doing.

What are one or two popular misconceptions about the services you provide and or some of the results that it produces?

Joe Pereira: The misconceptions are that if it's life insurance. I don't want to talk about life insurance. Are these things guaranteed? Does the government protect them? And I have to explain exactly where and why they are the best benefit for them.

Okay. What about annuities? Is there some misconception related to annuities?

Joe Pereira: Yes. The older the person is, they remember when an annuity was if they died, that was it.

Younger persons are starting to understand that you can have lifetime incomes being paid by annuities. A lot of elderly folks they still think it's for when you're alive and when you die there is nothing your beneficiary gets. That is starting to change with proper explaining.

What do you think is the main reason your ideal client might not hire you. Is there anything you can think of? Sort of address? Sort of like pre-addressing someone's concern.

Joe Pereira: I can't think of a reason on earth why they wouldn't do business with me.

Okay. All right. Well, then give us reasons why they should hire you. Let's put it that way then. Change it around.

Joe Pereira: Okay. I believe firmly that as we go through the process, because this is a four or five meeting process, that they will understand that I have their best interests in mind. My character and my reputation and the people who know me would probably be happy to tell them, yeah, Joe's a good guy. This is what he did for me.

Awesome. Okay, so if you get to meet with one of your ideal prospects, you talk about a multi-meeting process. Can you describe that in a little more detail ...

167

The process you're going to take a person through to learn about them and their goals and finances.

Joe Pereira: I have a meeting mandatory with wife and husband to sit down and just talk with them about why they came to my office or why they accepted my invitation and ask them to be as honest as possible, not hold back anything. It's so vital that I know everything about them and what their philosophy is. We then decide if we can work together with them. I give them a budget form to complete. I advise not to be a bookkeeper and make it to the penny but give me some round numbers to see how they're handling their money right now. Once the relationship has been established we go through the normal process .Depending on their age and such and figure out how they're going to get kids through college without losing my retirement money ... What's the best way to save and avoid taxes.

Then we go down through that. We find out what their long-term goals are after that and use their own budget to show where there might be using it in a better way. And then I present a plan to them and then go over that and ... -

Is that in the second meeting? I'm sorry, which meeting are we on?

Joe Pereira: Well, I've gone through a meeting with them, then they come back and discuss what we talked about when we had this general interview and I gave them a budget form to fill out. They fill out that budget form. They come back and go through that. I look to see for places that they're wasting money or can put it to better use. And then I develop a plan for them and then we discuss the plan.

Okay. All right, that sounds like a great detailed process in which you can discover specifically what someone needs and make recommendations on what they need to do. So what are the benefits that come from this type of process that someone's going get when they become your client and they go through this process. They take your recommendations, what are some of the benefits they're going to get from it?

Joe Pereira: Well, hopefully the biggest benefit they'll get is peace of mind and be prepared for the things that happen in life. The unexpected things that we've tried to build a protective wall around with access to funds in need of emergencies and not tied up in non-liquid assets.

Okay. You've been practicing for quite a long time, about thirty years you mentioned.

Joe Pereira: Yes, I hope to get it right soon. That's a practicing joke.

Yeah, exactly. After doing this so long, what's the biggest reason why you get up in the morning and go to work and still stay excited about it, because it's easy for people to get burned out after 30 years of doing something.

Joe Pereira: Every day that I get up, I have someone, somewhere down the line that I know I can help. And that's the reason.   Whether or not you want to put this in here, I honestly believe that God put me on the planet for a purpose and this is the purpose that I've been given.

Yeah, I believe that too. I believe we all have a purpose God has given us and it sounds like you are really focused on continuing to do that. You mentioned earlier, related to that, earlier in this interview you mentioned the importance of character when it comes to being an advisor. And I've talked to a lot of advisors and seen different things that they're doing and ... Of course we have the Bernie Madoff situation.

Joe Pereira: Yes.

It still stands like a dark shadow over the entire financial industry, even if you offer services and products that are nothing like money management. It can be

something completely different but if anyone thinks "financial services" they have this dark shadow.

So can you talk a little bit about the importance of character and what that means in today's world.

Joe Pereira: Well, I run my practice knowing you have to live a way that you can go to sleep every night, soundly. You never have to worry about what lie did you tell to somebody because you can't remember who you lied to or what it is. Character is just doing what's best for somebody else. Sometimes it's not the best for you but it's what's best for somebody else. That's the reason I'm in the business.

I think I sort of hear the golden rule coming through there-

Joe Pereira: If it's coming through, yes.

Do unto others what you would want them to do unto you.

Joe Pereira: Yes.

Love thy neighbor as thyself.

Joe Pereira: Was it Rodney Dangerfield who said "Do unto others before they do unto you?

I don't know but that sounds pretty funny. Well, hopefully ... I know you're not taking that attitude, but for me I hope no one takes that type of approach to their practice. What else would you like to share today, Joe? Anything else? Anything else that you can think of?

Joe Pereira: Actually, do the math. As I've been in business thirty years, I'm heading into the sunset and I still have to live with a conscious and I know all the people I've helped and I appreciate that and it keeps me going.

Well, it's been good today, Joe. I appreciate you spending this time with us and I found it really interesting to learn about your practice and how you work with your clients ... And I just wanted to say thanks -

Joe Pereira: I wanted to mention that I use the RetirementView software.

Yeah, well how's that helping out in your practice?

Joe Pereira: It's wonderful. It is really good. And I think that helps break some of the ice, trust ice. When they see it's numbers they put in, not numbers that I put in. That's the biggest thing to overcome.

So you do it live and in person with the client?

Joe Pereira: Yep.

Do you find that the clients generally understand what their picture is all about?

Joe Pereira: Yeah, and they really get surprised. A lot of them. And a lot of people still, after all these years, just don't understand that your social security could become a taxable event when you retire. They get shocked to learn about that.

The tax man cometh.

Joe Pereira: Yes.

I'm also a tax preparer.

You are?

Joe Pereira: That's where I get the majority of my clients from.

You do their taxes?

Joe Pereira: Yep. So I really have to see their tax returns and understand their finances.

Yeah, so you know all about their financial situation before you move into talking about these other services you do.

Joe Pereira: Most of the time I get referred by tax clients.

Okay, well. Anything else that you can think of that you would like to share?

Joe Pereira: I have a question. Going back to what really has me excited is this mortgage thing. Basically it's a function of a mortgage company but in association with and through Allianz Life Insurance Company. That's where the tax-free part comes in.

Okay.

Joe Pereira: Because one company I use has a life insurance plan that takes universal life and between those two it's amazing how fast they can pay off the mortgage and as long as they have the wherewithal to, and the discipline that once that mortgage is paid off, they keep sending in a mortgage payment as if they had a mortgage and it's going into the life insurance policy.

So they can just build up a really good addition to whatever they had for their retirement without spending up the extra money.

That sounds really interesting. Can you give us some basic information about it?

Joe Pereira: Sure. Here is an overview of how it works....

THE MORTGAGE KILLER PLAN

Everyone who has a 30 year mortgage should know that the price they bought their home for and what they really end up paying for it are two different amounts. This is due to the fact that the banks and lenders charge a staggering amount of interest up front. It is not uncommon for the total price you pay for your home to be twice the original cost. This system has limited your possibility of more efficient ways to finance your home because the traditional amortized loan makes large profits for them. The chart below shows how many years it takes before the principal payment amount is larger than the interest payment.

RATE	YEARS
5.00 %	16.3
4.50 %	14.8
4.00 %	12.5
3.75 %	11.5
3.50 %	10.3

Consider how much brighter your financial future would be if you saved a large part of the interest the bank is collecting and you used it to create a savings plan that could grow tax deferred without any stock market risk. Consider how much more equity you would have in your home if for some reason you had to sell it.

The Mortgage Killer approach combines financial products and strategies usually available only as separate products. When they are combined in this plan your financial future will grow unbelievably by implementing the program as it is designed.

By utilizing a unique loan to finance your home, combining it with a special checking account like the one you currently have plus an insurance product, the growth engine will astound you. When grouped together, this strategy will save tens of thousands in interest payments, speed up the growth of accessible equity in your home, pay off your home incredibly sooner while all the time increasing your insured private reserve account. This account has real growth potential without market risk, is tax deferred, can be accessed for tax free income and provide long term care benefits. Each part of the strategy is important for success.

THE CHECKING ACCOUNT

Most Americans manage their daily lives and finances by use of a checking account. The bank acts as a temporary storage place to deposit your income and pay your expenses. These checking accounts offer no or very low interest rates on the balances. The reserve checking account uses these dollars to work for you by combining the checking account with your mortgage loan. This creates a method whereby your borrowing and your banking use the deposits to lower your principal balance. This in turn lowers your interest payments which are calculated daily. Saved interest is equal to interest earned. This checking account provides all of the same functions of your current checking account including 24/7 banking access, ATM cards, check writing and online bill paying.

AN INTEREST ONLY 30 YEAR EQUITY LINE OF CREDIT

This is the financing method used in many countries outside of the United States. It has been available in the United States since 2005 but the lending institutions have not supported it. This is mainly because of the amount of interest they lose. With an interest only loan your monthly mortgage payment will be less than your current amortized loan. This in turn has the saved interest to be deposited into your insured private reserve account.

During the time your funds are sitting in the checking account that amount is credited against the principal balance. Since interest is computed daily on the principal balance this lowers the interest being calculated until you need to use the checking account. After you have paid all of your monthly bills the balance is credited against the principal. This cycle continues for each month. This method accelerates the reduction of your principal and increases your equity. There are additional tax benefits that are discussed later.

Most people would be interested in making additional payments whenever possible to pay off the mortgage except for the fact those funds come out of their lifestyle and become illiquid as part of their equity. If emergency funds are needed, they have to apply for a loan. This is not the case with this program. The reserve funds are totally liquid. The Mortgage Killer method allows for emergencies to be paid by writing a check from the zero balance account. This unique plan pays off your home sooner but at the same time conserves your liquidity.

THE PRIVATE RESERVE ACCOUNT

The insured private reserve account provides for you to automatically place the interest saved on your new loan into a tax advantaged plan. The tax advantaged insured private reserve account is allowed by the IRS through IRC 7702 and IRC72(e) of the Internal Revenue Code. In addition to the tax advantage the account has competitive rates of return without stock market risk, retirement income protection and long term care benefits. Properly constructed it can be a tax free account. This would reduce income taxes in retirement and lower the amount of Social Security that would be taxed.

The major benefit of the Mortgage Killer is that for the same dollars you are currently paying for your amortized loan you could become financially independent when you retire.

The example Comparison Chart below is based on a 43 year old male with a $290,000 mortgage balance in year four of a 30 year mortgage, a combined monthly income of $8,000, monthly expenses of $4,500 not including $1,549 principal and interest on their current mortgage.

Summary of The Smart Mortgage Plan

Prepared for: John Sample
Advisor: Joseph Pereira

Mortgage Comparison

Year	Current Traditional Mortgage			Smart Mortgage Loan		
	Mortgage Balance	Cumulative Interest Paid	Estimated Equity	Mortgage Balance	Estimated Equity	Smart Mortgage Strategy Increase in Equity
1	$309,208	$11,714	$84,542	$251,684	$132,065	$47,544
2	$303,195	$23,206	$98,430	$230,326	$171,299	$72,868
3	$296,952	$34,469	$112,705	$199,448	$210,210	$97,504
4	$290,471	$45,495	$127,379	$168,535	$249,315	$121,935
5	$283,744	$56,272	$142,464	$137,051	$289,156	$146,692
6	$276,759	$66,794	$157,973	$104,408	$330,323	$172,350
7	$269,508	$77,048	$173,919	$69,945	$373,481	$199,563
8	$261,980	$87,026	$190,315	$32,698	$419,397	$229,082
9	$254,165	$96,717	$207,176	$0	$461,341	$254,165
10	$246,052	$106,110	$224,516	$0	$470,568	$246,052
15	$200,601	$148,187	$318,944	$0	$519,545	$200,601
20	$145,792	$180,908	$427,627	$0	$573,619	$145,792
25	$79,700	$202,344	$553,623	$0	$633,322	$79,700
30	$0	$210,172	$699,239	$0	$699,239	$0

Interest Saved on All in One Loan	$133,286

Estimated Number of Years to Pay Off Mortgage	9

Equity assumes an estimate appreciation rate on the property based upon your specific area and is only estimated. As a result the equity shown may be higher or lower depending upon the appreciation rate used.

Monthly savings in P&I payment which is directed to the Private Reserve Acct	$539

Payment to the Private Reserve Account Once the Loan is Paid Off	$1,459

Private Reserve Account

Year	Age	IUL Accumulation Value	IUL Cash Surrender Value	The Smart Mortgage Private Reserve Account	Future Value of Term Costs
1	44	$4,346	$0	$4,346	$0
2	45	$8,983	$0	$8,983	$0
3	46	$13,923	$4,115	$13,923	$0
4	47	$19,185	$9,517	$19,185	$0
5	48	$24,802	$15,280	$24,802	$0
6	49	$30,807	$21,433	$30,807	$0
7	50	$37,225	$29,728	$37,225	$0
8	51	$44,076	$38,453	$44,076	$0
9	52	$51,364	$47,638	$51,364	$0
10	53	$59,927	$68,053	$59,927	$0
15	58	$197,336	$197,336	$197,336	$0
20	63	$381,916	$381,916	$381,916	$0
25	68	$648,994	$648,994	$648,994	$0
30	73	$1,001,487	$1,031,487	$1,031,487	$0

Total Savings at Age	95	$5,612,805
Death Benefit at Age	95	$5,929,605

Mortgages Offered Through CMG Financial NMLS #271003

Disclaimer

The financial benefits as shown in the Comparison Chart are dependent upon the performance of the life insurance companies product associated with the program. All benefits and claims paying ability are dependent upon the company's financial ability to pay.

Some of the benefits shown are based on the past history of the S & P 500 Index performance.

Tim Turner: Thanks for sharing that information, Joe. And thanks for taking the time to share your insights and expertise as well.

Joe Pereira: Glad to do it, Tim. I enjoyed it. Thanks for taking the time to put this together.

Tim Turner: You're welcome Joe.

CONTACT INFORMATION:

Joseph Pereira
10300 SW 72 St. Suite 470J
Miami, FL 33173
Phone: (305) 598-3180
Email: mrjoe1836@netzero.net
Website: http://www.mortgagekiller.expert

Made in the USA
Lexington, KY
23 February 2018